Granville Barker's
Prefaces to Shakespeare

# THE MERCHANT
# OF VENICE

Foreword by
Richard Eyre

D1464896

First published in this collected paperback edition in 1993 jointly by
Nick Hern Books Limited, 14 Larden Road, London W3 7ST
and the Royal National Theatre, London,
by arrangement with Batsford.

*Preface to The Merchant of Venice.* Originally published in 1923

Copyright © the Estate of Harley Granville Barker 1993

Foreword copyright © Richard Eyre 1993

Set in 10/11 Baskerville by Pure Tech Corporation, Pondicherry
(India)
Printed in Australia by
Australian Print Group

A CIP catalogue record for this book is available from the British
Library

ISBN 1 85459 110 X

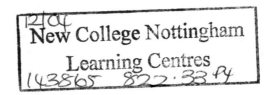

# Shakespeare Alive!

The history of the theatre in England in this century can be told largely through the lives and work of two men: George Bernard Shaw and Harley Granville Barker, a triple-barrelled cadence of names that resonates like the ruffling of the pages of a large book in a silent public library. One was a brilliant polemicist who dealt with certainties and assertions and sometimes, but not often enough, breathed life into his sermons; the other a committed sceptic who started from the premise that the only thing certain about human behaviour was that nothing was certain. Both, however, possessed a passionate certainty about the importance of the theatre and the need to revise its form, its content, and the way that it was managed. Shaw was a playwright, critic and pamphleteer, Barker a playwright, director and actor.

*The Voysey Inheritance* is, at least in my opinion, Granville Barker's best play: a complex web of family relationships, a fervent but never unambiguous indictment of a world dominated by the mutually dependent obsessions of greed, class, and self-deception. It's also a virtuoso display of stagecraft: the writer showing that as director he can handle twelve speaking characters on stage at one time, and that as actor he can deal with the most ambitious and unexpected modulations of thought and feeling. The 'inheritance' of the Voyseys is a legacy of debt, bad faith, and bitter family dissension. Edward's father has, shortly before his death, revealed that he has been cheating the family firm of solicitors for many years, as his father had for many years before that. Towards the end of the play Edward Voysey, the youngest son, confronts the woman he loves:

EDWARD.    Why wouldn't he own the truth to me about himself?

BEATRICE.    Perhaps he took care not to know it. Would you have understood?

EDWARD.    Perhaps not. But I loved him.

BEATRICE.    That would silence a bench of judges.

Shaw would have used the story to moralise and polemicise. He might have had the son hate the father; he might have had him forgive him; he might have had him indict him as a paradigm of capitalism; he would never have said he loved him.

Everybody needs a father, or, failing that, a father-figure. He may be a teacher, a prophet, a boss, a priest perhaps, a political leader, a friend, or, sometimes, if you are very lucky, the real one. If you can't find a father you must invent him. In some ways, not altogether trivial, Granville Barker is something of a father-figure for me. He's a writer whom I admire more than any twentieth-century English writer before the sixties – Chekhov with an English accent; he's the first modern British director; he's the real founder of the National Theatre and, in his *Prefaces*, he's a man who, alone amongst Shakespearean commentators before Jan Kott, believed in the power of Shakespeare on stage.

There was a myth that Granville Barker was the natural son of Shaw. He was certainly someone whom Shaw could, in his awkward way, cherish and admire, educate and castigate. When Barker fell wildly in love ('in the Italian manner' as Shaw said) with Helen Huntington, an American millionairess, he married her, acquired a hyphen in his surname, moved first to Devon to play the part of a country squire, and then to France to a life of seclusion. Shaw thought that he had buried himself alive and could never reconcile himself to the loss. It was, as his biographer

Hesketh Pearson said: 'The only important matter about which he asked me to be reticent.'

After directing many of Shaw's plays for many years, acting many of his best roles (written by Shaw with Barker in mind), dreaming and planning together the birth of a National Theatre, not to mention writing, directing, and acting in his own plays while managing his own company at the Royal Court, Barker withdrew from the theatre, and for twenty years there was silence between the two men. Only on the occasion of the death of Shaw's wife did they communicate by letters. 'I did not know I could be so moved by anything,' wrote Shaw to him.

Out of this self-exile came one major work, slowly assembled over many years: *The Prefaces to Shakespeare*. With a few exceptions (Auden on *Othello*, Barbara Everett on *Hamlet*, Jan Kott on *The Tempest*) it's the only critical work about Shakespeare that's made any impact on me, apart, that is, from my father's view of Shakespeare, which was brief and brutal: 'It's absolute balls.'

As much as we need a good father, we need a good teacher. Mine, improbably perhaps, was Kingsley Amis. He'd arrived, somewhat diffidently, at Cambridge at the same time as I did. The depth of my ignorance of English literature corresponded almost exactly to his dislike of the theatre. Nevertheless, he made me see Shakespeare with a mind uncontaminated by the views of academics, whom he would never have described as his fellows and whose views he regarded as, well, academic. I would write essays marinated in the opinions of Spurgeon, Wilson Knight, Dover Wilson and a large cast of critical supernumeraries. He would gently, but courteously, cast aside my essay about, say, *Twelfth Night*: 'But what do *you* think of this play? Do you think it's any good?' 'Well ... er ... it's Shakespeare.' 'Yes, but is it any *good*? I mean as a *play*. It says it's a comedy. Fine. But does it have any decent jokes?'

I took this for irreverence, heresy even. Over the years, however, I've come to regard this as good teaching, or, closely allied, good direction. It's asking the right questions, unintimidated by reputation, by tradition, by received opinion, or by critical orthodoxy. This was shocking, but healthy, for a young and impressionable man ripe to become a fundamentalist in matters of literary taste and ready to revere F. R. Leavis as the Ayatollah of 'Cambridge English'. What you have is yourself and the text, only that. That's the lesson of Granville Barker: 'We have the text to guide us, half a dozen stage directions, and that is all. I abide by the text and the demands of the text and beyond that I claim freedom.' I can't imagine a more useful and more enduring dictum.

*The Prefaces* have a practical aim: 'I want to see Shakespeare made fully effective on the English stage. That is the best sort of help I can lend.' What Granville Barker wrote is a primer for directors and actors working on the plays of Shakespeare. There is lamentably little useful literature about the making of theatre, even though there is an indigestible glut of memoirs and biographies, largely concerned with events that have taken place *after* the curtain has fallen. If I was asked by a visiting Martian to recommend books which would help him, her or it to make theatre in the manner of the European I could only offer four books: Stanislavsky on *The Art of the Stage*, John Willett's *Brecht on Theatre*, Peter Brook's *The Empty Space*, and *The Prefaces to Shakespeare*.

Stanislavsky offers a pseudo-scientific dissection of the art of acting which is, in some respects, like reading Freud on the mechanism of the joke: earnest, well-meaning, but devoid of the indispensable ingredient of its subject matter: humour. Stanislavsky's great contribution was to demand that actors hold the mirror up to nature, that they take their craft as seriously as the writers they served, and to provide some sort of formal discipline within which both aims could be realised.

Brecht provided a manifesto that was a political and aesthetic response to the baroque encrustations of the scenery-laden, star-dominated, archaic boulevard theatre of Germany in the twenties. Although much of what he wrote as theory is an unpalatable mix of political ideology and artistic instruction, it is his theatrical instinct that prevails. He asserts, he insists, he browbeats. He demands that the stage, like society, must be re-examined, reformed, that the audience's habits mustn't be satisfied, they must be changed, but just when he is about to nail his 13 Articles to the church door he drops the voice of the zealot: 'The stage is not a hothouse or a zoological museum full of stuffed animals. It must be peopled with live, three-dimensional self-contradictory people with their passions, unconsidered utterances and actions.' In all art forms, he says, the guardians of orthodoxy will assert that there are eternal and immutable laws that you ignore at your peril, but in the theatre there is only one inflexible rule: 'The proof of the pudding is in the eating.' Brecht teaches us to ask the question: what goes on in a theatre?

Brook takes that question even further: what *is* theatre? It's a philosophical, but eminently practical, question that Brook has been asking for over 30 years and which has taken him to the African desert, a quarry in Iran, and an abandoned music hall in Paris. 'I take an empty space and call it a bare stage. A man walks across this empty space while someone else is watching him, and that is all that is needed for an act of theatre to be engaged.' For all his apparent concern with metaphyics, there is no more practical man of the theatre than Brook.

I was once at a seminar where someone asked him what was the job of the director. 'To get the actors on and off stage,' he said. Like Brecht, like Stanislavsky, like Granville Barker, Brook argues that for the theatre to be expressive it must be, above all, simple and unaffected: a distillation of language, of gesture, of action, of design, where meaning is the essence. The meaning must be felt as much as understood. 'They don't have to understand with their ears,' says Granville Barker, 'just with their guts.'

Brecht did not acknowledge a debt to Granville Barker. Perhaps he was not aware of one, but it seems to me that Barker's Shakespeare productions were the direct antecedents of Brecht's work. He certainly knew enough about English theatre to know that he was on to a good thing adapting *The Beggar's Opera*, *The Recruiting Officer* and *Coriolanus*. Brecht has been lauded for destroying illusionism; Granville Barker has been unhymned. He aimed at re-establishing the relationship between actor and audience that had existed in Shakespeare's theatre – and this at a time when the prevailing style of Shakespearean production involved *not* stopping short of having live sheep in *As You Like It*. He abolished footlights and the proscenium arch, building out an apron over the orchestra pit which Shaw said 'apparently trebled the spaciousness of the stage. . . . To the imagination it looks as if he had invented a new heaven and a new earth.'

His response to staging Shakespeare was not to look for a synthetic Elizabethanism. 'We shall not save our souls by being Elizabethan.' To recreate the Globe would, he knew, be aesthetic anasthaesia, involving the audience in an insincere conspiracy to pretend that they were willing collaborators in a vain effort to turn the clock back. His answers to staging Shakespeare were similar to Brecht's for *his* plays and, in some senses, to

Chekhov's for his. He wanted scenery not to decorate and be literal, but to be expressive and metaphorical, and at the same time, in apparent contradiction, to be specific and be real, while being minimal and iconographic: the cart in *Mother Courage*, the nursery in *The Cherry Orchard*, the dining table in *The Voysey Inheritance*. 'To create a new hieroglyphic language of scenery. That, in a phrase, is the problem. If the designer finds himself competing with the actors, the sole interpreters Shakespeare has licensed, then it is he that is the intruder and must retire.'

In *The Prefaces* Granville Barker argues for a fluency of staging unbroken by scene changes. Likewise the verse should be spoken fast. 'Be swift, be swift, be not poetical,' he wrote on the dressing-room mirror of Cathleen Nesbitt when she played Perdita. Within the speed, however, detailed reality. *Meaning* above all.

It is the director's task, with the actors, to illuminate the meanings of a play: its vocabulary, its syntax, and its philosophy. The director has to ask what each scene is revealing about the characters and their actions: what story is each scene telling us? In *The Prefaces* Granville Barker exhumes, examines and explains the lost stagecraft of Shakespeare line by line, scene by scene, play by play.

Directing Shakespeare is a matter of understanding the meaning of a scene and staging it in the light of that knowledge. Easier said than done, but it's at the heart of the business of directing any play, and directing Shakespeare is merely directing writ large. Beyond that, as David Mamet has observed, 'choice of actions and adverbs constitute the craft of directing'. Get up from that chair and walk across the room. Slowly.

With Shakespeare as with any other playwright the director's job is to make the play live, now, in the present tense. 'Spontaneous enjoyment is the life of the theatre,' says Granville Barker in his Preface to *Love's Labour's Lost*. To receive a review, as Granville Barker did, headed *SHAKESPEARE ALIVE!* is the most, but should be the least, that a director must hope for.

I regard Granville Barker not only as the first modern English director but as the most influential. Curiously, partly as a result of his early withdrawal from the theatre, partly because his *Prefaces* have been out of print for many years, and partly because of his own self-effacement, he has been unjustly ignored both in the theatre and in the academic world, where the codification of their 'systems' has resulted in the canonisation of Brecht and Stanislavsky. I hope the re-publication of *The Prefaces* will right the balance. Granville Barker himself always thought of them as his permanent legacy to the theatre.

My sense of filial identification is not entirely a professional one. When I directed *The Voysey Inheritance* I wanted a photograph of the author on the poster. A number of people protested that it was the height, or depth, of vanity and self-aggrandisement to put my own photograph on the poster. I was astonished, I was bewildered, but I was not unflattered. I still can't see the resemblance, but it's not through lack of trying.

Two years ago the Royal National Theatre was presented with a wonderful bronze bust of Granville Barker by Katherine Scott (the wife, incidentally, of the Antarctic hero). For a while it sat on the windowsill of my office like a benign household god. Then it was installed on a bracket in the foyer opposite a bust of Olivier, the two men eyeing each other in wary mutual regard. A few months later it was stolen; an act of homage perhaps. I miss him.

**Richard Eyre**

# Introduction

We have still much to learn about Shakespeare the playwright. Strange that it should be so, after three centuries of commentary and performance, but explicable. For the Procrustean methods of a changed theatre deformed the plays, and put the art of them to confusion; and scholars, with this much excuse, have been apt to divorce their Shakespeare from the theatre altogether, to think him a poet whose use of the stage was quite incidental, whose glory had small relation to it, for whose lapses it was to blame.

## The Study and the Stage

THIS much is to be said for Garrick and his predecessors and successors in the practice of reshaping Shakespeare's work to the theatre of their time. The essence of it was living drama to them, and they meant to keep it alive for their public. They wanted to avoid whatever would provoke question and so check that spontaneity of response upon which acted drama depends. Garrick saw the plays, with their lack of 'art', through the spectacles of contemporary culture; and the bare Elizabethan stage, if it met his mind's eye at all, doubtless as a barbarous makeshift. Shakespeare was for him a problem; he tackled it, from our point of view, misguidedly and with an overplus of enthusiasm. His was a positive world; too near in time, moreover, as well as too opposed in taste to Shakespeare's to treat it perspectively. The romantic movement might have brought a more concordant outlook. But by then the scholars were off their own way; while the theatre began to think of its Shakespeare from the point of view of the picturesque, and, later, in terms of upholstery. Nineteenth-century drama developed along the lines of realistic illusion, and the staging of Shakespeare was further subdued to this, with inevitably disastrous effect on the speaking of his verse; there was less perversion of text perhaps, but actually more wrenching of the construction of the plays for the convenience of the stage carpenter. The public appetite for this sort of thing having been gorged, producers then turned to newer—and older—contrivances, leaving 'realism' (so called) to the modern comedy that had fathered it. Amid much vaporous theorizing—but let us humbly own how hard it is not to write nonsense about art, which seems ever pleading to be enjoyed and not written about at all—the surprising discovery had been made that varieties of stagecraft and stage were not historical accidents but artistic obligations, that Greek drama belonged in a Greek theatre, that Elizabethan plays, therefore, would, presumably, do best upon an Elizabethan stage, that there was nothing sacrosanct about scenery, footlights, drop-curtain or any of their belongings. This brings us to the present situation.

There are few enough Greek theatres in which Greek tragedy can be played; few enough people want to see it, and they will applaud it encouragingly however it is done. Some acknowledgement is due to the altruism of the doers! Shakespeare is another matter. The English theatre, doubtful of its destiny, of necessity venal, opening its doors to all comers, seems yet, as by some instinct, to seek renewal of strength in him. An actor, unless success has made him cynical, or his talent be merely trivial, may take some pride in the hall mark of Shakespearean achievement. So may a manager if he thinks he can afford it. The public (or their spokesmen) seem to consider Shakespeare and his genius a sort of national property, which, truly, they do nothing to conserve, but in which they have moral rights not lightly to be flouted. The production of the plays is thus still apt to be marked by a timid respect for 'the usual thing'; their acting is crippled by pseudo-traditions, which are inert because they are not Shakespearean at all. They are the accumulation of two centuries of progressive misconception and distortion of his playwright's art. On the other hand, England has been spared production of Shakespeare according to this or that even more irrelevant theory of presentationalism, symbolism, constructivism or what not. There is the breach in the wall of 'realism', but we have not yet made up our minds to pass through, taking our Shakespeare with us.

Incidentally, we owe the beginning of the breach to Mr William Poel, who, with fanatical courage, when 'realism' was at the tottering height of its triumph in the later revivals of Sir Henry Irving, and the yet more richly upholstered revelations of Sir Herbert Tree, thrust the Elizabethan stage in all its apparent eccentricity upon our unwilling notice.' Mr Poel shook complacency. He could not expect to do much more; for he was a logical reformer. He showed us the Elizabethan stage, with Antony and Cleopatra, Troilus and Cressida, in their ruffs and farthingales as for Shakespeare's audiences they lived. Q.E.D. There, however, as far as the popular theatre was concerned, the matter seemed to rest for twenty years or so. But it was just such a demonstration that was needed; anything less drastic and provocative might have been passed over with mild approval.

To get the balance true, let us admit that while Shakespeare was an Elizabethan playwright he was—and now is to us—predominantly something much more. Therefore we had better not too unquestioningly thrust him back within the confines his genius has escaped, nor presume him to have felt the pettier circumstances of his theatre sacrosanct. Nor can we turn Elizabethans as we watch the plays; and every mental effort to do so will subtract from our enjoyment of them. This is the case against the circumstantial reproduction of Shakespeare's staging. But Mr Poel's achievement remains; he cleared for us from Shakespeare's stagecraft the scenic rubbish by which it had been so long encumbered and disguised. And we could now, if we would, make a promising fresh start. For the scholars, on their side, have lately—the scholarly among them—cut clear of the transcendental fog (scenic illusion of another sort) in which their nine-teenth-century peers loved to lose themselves, and they too are beginning again at the beginning. A text acquires virtue now by its claim to be a prompt book, and the most comprehensive work of our time upon the Elizabe-than stage is an elaborate sorting-out of plays, companies and theatres. On Dr Pollard's treatment of the texts and on the foundations of fact laid by Sir Edmund Chambers a new scholarship is rising, aiming first to see Shakes-peare in the theatre for which he wrote. It is a scholar-ship, therefore, by which the theatre of today can profit, to which, by its acting of Shakespeare, it could contrib-ute, one would hope. Nor should the scholars disdain the help; for criticism cannot live upon criticism, it needs refreshment from the living art. Besides, what is all the criticism and scholarship finally for if not to keep Shakes-peare alive? And he must always be most alive—even if roughly and rudely alive—in the theatre. Let the scholars force a way in there, if need be. Its fervid atmosphere will do them good; the benefit will be mu-tual.

These Prefaces are an attempt to profit by this new scholarship and to contribute to it some research into Shakespeare's stagecraft, by examining the plays, one after another, in the light of the interpretation he designed for them, so far as this can be deduced; to discover, if possible, the production he would have desired for them, all merely incidental circumstances apart. They might profit more written a generation hence, for the ground they build upon is still far from clear. And this introduction is by no means a conspectus of the subject; that can only come as a sequel. There has been, in this branch of Shakespearean study, too much generalization and far too little analysis of material.[2]

## Shakespeare's Stagecraft

SHAKESPEARE'S own career was not a long one. The whole history of the theatre he wrote for does not cover a century. Between Marlowe and Massinger, from the first blaze to the glowing of the embers, it is but fifty years. Yet even while Shakespeare was at work, the stage to which he fitted his plays underwent constant and perhaps radical change. From Burbage's first theatre to the Globe, then to Blackfriars, not to mention excursions to Court and into the great halls—change of audiences and their behaviour, of their taste, development of the art of acting, change of the stage itself and its resources were all involved in the progress, and are all, we may be sure, reflected to some degree in the plays themselves. We guess at the conditions of each sort of stage and theatre, but there is often the teasing question to which of them had a play, as we have it now, been adapted. And of the 'private' theatre, most in vogue for the ten years preceding the printing of the First Folio so far we know least. The dating of texts and their ascription to the usages of a particular theatre may often be a searchlight upon their stagecraft. Here is much work for the new scholarship.

Conversely, the watchful working-out of the plays in action upon this stage or that would be of use to the scholars, who otherwise must reconstruct their theatre and gloss their texts as in a vacuum. The play was once fitted to the stage; it is by no means impossible to rebuild that stage now, with its doors, balconies, curtains and machines, by measuring the needs of the play. It is idle, for instance, to imagine scenes upon inner or upper stage without evidence that they will be audible or visible there; and editing is still vitiated by lack of this simple knowledge. Here, if nowhere else, this present research must fall short, for its method should rightly be experimental; more than one mind should be at work on it, moreover.

The text of a play is a score waiting performance, and the performance and its preparation are, almost from the beginning, a work of collaboration. A producer may direct the preparation, certainly. But if he only knows how to give orders, he has mistaken his vocation; he had better be a drill-sergeant. He might talk to his company when they all met together for the first time to study *Love's Labour's Lost, Julius Cæsar* or *King Lear*, on some such lines as these Prefaces pursue, giving a considered opinion of the play, drawing a picture of it in action, providing, in fact, a hypothesis which mutual study would prove—and might partly disprove. No sort of study of a play can better the preparation of its performance if this is rightly done. The matured art of the playwright lies in giving life to characters in action, and the secret of it in giving each character a due chance in the battle, the action of a play becoming literally the fighting of a battle of character. So the greater the playwright, the wider and deeper his sympathies, the more genuine this opposition will be and the less easily will a single mind grasp it, as it must be grasped, in the fullness of its emotion. The dialogue of a play runs—and often intricately—upon lines of reason, but it is charged besides with an emotion which speech releases, yet only releases fully when the speaker is—as an actor is—identified with the character. There is further the incidental action, implicit in the dialogue, which springs to life only when a scene is in being. A play, in fact, as we find it written, is a magic spell; and even the magician cannot always foresee the full effect of it.

Not every play, it must be owned, will respond to such intensive study. Many, ambitiously conceived, would collapse under the strain. Many are mere occasions for display of their actors' wit or eloquence, good looks or nice behaviour, and meant to be no more; and if they are skilfully contrived the parts fit together and the whole machine should go like clockwork. Nor, in fact, are even the greatest plays often so studied. There is hardly a theatre in the world where masterpiece and trumpery alike are not rushed through rehearsals to an arbitrarily effective performance, little more learned of them than the words, gaps in the understanding of them filled up with 'business'—effect without cause, the demand for this being the curse of the theatre as of other arts, as of other things than art. Not to such treatment will the greater plays of Shakespeare yield their secrets. But working upon a stage which reproduced the essential conditions of his, working as students, not as showmen merely, a company of actors might well find many of the riddles of the library answering themselves unasked. And these Prefaces could best be a record of such work, if such work were to be done.

We cannot, on the other hand, begin our research by postulating the principles of the Elizabethan stage. One is tempted to say it had none, was too much a child of nature to bother about such things. Principles were doubtless imposed upon it when it reached respectability, and heads would be bowed to the yoke. Shakespeare's among them? He had served a most practical apprenticeship to his trade. If he did not hold horses at the door, he sat behind the curtains, we may be sure, and held the prompt book on occasion. He acted, he cobbled other men's plays, he could write his own to order. Such a one may stay a journeyman if he is not a genius, but he will not become a doctrinaire. Shakespeare's work shows such principles as the growth of a tree shows. It is not haphazard merely because it is not formal; it is shaped by inner strength. The theatre, as he found it, allowed him and encouraged him to great freedom of development. Because the material resources of a stage are simple, it does not follow that the technique of its playwriting will stay so. Crude work may show up more crudely, when there are none of the fal-lals of illusion to disguise it that the modern theatre provides. But, if he has it in him, a dramatist can, so unfettered, develop the essentials of his art more boldly and more subtly too. The Elizabethan drama made an amazingly quick advance from crudity to an excellence which was often technically most elaborate. The advance and the not less amazing gulf which divides its best from its worst may be ascribed to the simplicity of the machinery it employed. That its decadence was precipitated by the influence of the Masque and the shifting of its centre of interest from the barer public stage to the candle-lit private theatre, where the machinery of the Masque became effective, it would be rash to assert; but the occurrences are suspiciously related. Man and machine (here at any rate is a postulate, if a platitude!) are false allies in the theatre, secretly at odds; and when man gets the worst of it, drama is impoverished; and the struggle, we may add, is perennial. No great drama depends upon pageantry. All great drama tends to concentrate upon character; and, even so, not upon picturing men as they show themselves to the world like figures on a stage—though that is how it must ostensibly show them—but on the hidden man. And the progress of Shakespeare's art from *Love's Labour's Lost* to *Hamlet*, and thereafter with a difference, lies in the simplifying of this paradox and the solving of the problem it presents; and the process involves the developing of a very subtle sort of stagecraft indeed.

For one result we have what we may call a very self-contained drama. Its chief values, as we know, have not changed with the fashions of the theatre. It relies much on the music of the spoken word, and a company of schoolchildren with pleasant voices, and an ear for rhythm, may vociferate through a play to some effect. It is as much to be enjoyed in the reading, if we hear it in imagination as we read, as drama meant to be acted can be. As with its simplicities then, so it should be, we presume, with its complexities. The subtly emotional use of verse and the interplay of motive and character, can these not be appreciated apart from the bare boards of their original setting? It does not follow. It neither follows that the advantages of the Elizabethan stage were wholly negative nor that, with our present knowledge, we can imagine the full effect of a play in action upon it. The imagining of a play in action is, under no circumstances, an easy thing.[3] What would one not give to go backward through the centuries to see the first performance of *Hamlet*, played as Shakespeare had it played![4] In default, if we could but make ourselves read it as if it were a manuscript fresh from its author's hands! There is much to be said for turning one's back on the editors, even, when possible, upon the First Folio with its demarcation of acts and scenes, in favour of the Quartos—Dr Pollard's 'good' Quartos—in their yet greater simplicity.

# The Convention of Place

IT is, for instance, hard to discount the impression made merely by reading: *Scene i—Elsinore. A platform before the Castle*; and most of us have, to boot, early memories of painted battlements and tenth-century castles (of ageing Hamlets and their portly mothers for that matter) very difficult to dismiss. No great harm, one protests; it was a help, perhaps, to the unimaginative. But it is a first step to the certain misunderstanding of Shakespeare's stagecraft. The 'if, how and when' of the presenting of localities on the Elizabethan stage is, of course, a complex question. Shakespeare himself seems to have followed, consciously, no principles in the matter, nor was his practice very logical, nor at all consistent. It may vary with the play he is writing and the particular stage he is writing for; it will best be studied in relation to each play. We can, however, free ourselves from one general misconception which belongs to our own over-logical standpoint. When we learn with a shock of surprise—having begun in the schoolroom upon the Shakespeare of the editors, it comes as belated news to us—that neither battlements, throne rooms nor picturesque churchyards were to be seen at the Globe, and that *Elsinore. A platform before the Castle* is not Shakespeare at all, we yet imagine ourselves among the audience there busily conjuring these things up before the eye of faith. The Elizabethan audience was at no such pains. Nor was this their alternative to seeing the actors undisguisedly concerned with the doors, curtains and balconies which, by the play's requirements, should have been anything but what they were. As we, when a play has no hold on us, may fall to thinking about the scenery, so to a Globe audience, unmoved, the stage might be an obvious bare stage. But are we conscious of the scenery behind the actor when the play really moves us? If we are, there is something very wrong with the scenery, which should know its place as a background. The audience was not conscious of curtain and balcony when Burbage played Hamlet to them. They were conscious of Hamlet. That conventional background faded as does our painted illusion, and they certainly did not deliberately conjure up in its place mental pictures of Elsinore. The genus audience is passive, if expectant, imaginatively lazy till roused, never, one may be sure, at pains to make any effort that is generally unnecessary to enjoyment.

With Shakespeare the locality of a scene has dramatic importance, or it has none; and this is as true of his early plays as his late ones. Both in *Richard II* and *Antony and Cleopatra*, scene after scene passes with no exact indication of where we may be. With *Cleopatra* we are surely in Egypt, with Cæsar in Rome. Pompey appears, and the talk tells us that both Egypt and Rome are elsewhere; but positively where Pompey is at the moment we never learn.[5] Indoors or outdoors? The action of the scene or the clothing of the characters will tell us this if we need to know. But, suddenly transported to the Parthian war, our whereabouts is made amply plain. It is, however, made plain by allusion. The information peeps out through talk of kindred things; we are hardly aware we are being told, and, again, we learn no more than we need to learn. This, truly, is a striking development from the plump and plain

> Barkloughly Castle call they this at hand?

*of Richard II*, even from the more descriptive

> I am a stranger here in Gloucestershire:
> These high wild hills and rough, uneven ways
> Draw out our miles. . .

by which Shakespeare pictures and localizes the manoeuvres of Richard and Bolingbroke when he wants to.
But the purpose is the same, and the method essentially
the same.[6] Towards the end of the later play come scene
after scene of the marching and countermarching of
armies, of fighting, of truce, all the happenings of three
days' battle. Acts III and IV contain twenty-eight scenes
long and short; some of them are very short; three of
them have but four lines apiece. The editors conscien-
tiously ticket them *A plain near Actium, Another part of the
plain, Another part of the plain* and so on, and conclude that
Shakespeare is really going too far and too fast, is indeed
(I quote Sir Edmund Chambers) 'in some danger of
outrunning the apprehensions of his auditory.' Indeed he
might be if this cinematographic view of his intentions
were the right one! But it utterly falsifies them. Show an
audience such a succession of painted scenes—if you
could at the pace required—and they would give attention to nothing else whatever; the drama would pass
unnoticed. Had Shakespeare tried to define the whereabouts of every scene in any but the baldest phrases—the
protesting editors seem not to see that he makes no
attempt to; only *they* do!—he would have had to lengthen
and complicate them; had he written only a labelling
line or two he would still have distracted his audience
from the essential drama. Ignoring whereabouts, letting
it at most transpire when it naturally will, the characters
capture all attention. This is the true gain of the bare
stage; unless to some dramatic end no precious words
need be spent, in complying with the undramatic demands of space and time; incarnation of character can
be all in all. Given such a crisis as this the gain is yet
greater. We are carried through the phases of the three
days' battle; and what other stage convention would
allow us so varied a view of it, could so isolate the true

drama of it? For do we not pass through such a crisis in reality with just that indifference to time and place? These scenes, in their kind, show Shakespeare's stagecraft, not at its most reckless, but at its very best, and exemplify perfectly the freedom he enjoyed that the stage of visual illusion has inevitably lost. His drama is attached solely to its actors and their acting; that, perhaps, puts it in a phrase. They carry place and time with them as they move. The modern theatre still accepts the convention that measures time more or less by a play's convenience; a half-hour stands for an hour or more, and we never question the vagary. It was no more strange to an Elizabethan audience to see a street in Rome turned, in the use made of it, to the Senate House by the drawing of a curtain and the disclosure of Cæsar's state, to find Cleopatra's Monument now on the upper stage because Antony had to be drawn up to it, later on the lower because Cleopatra's death-scene could best be played there; it would seem that they were not too astonished even when Juliet, having taken leave of Romeo on the balcony of her bedroom and watched him descend to the lower stage, the scene continuing, came down, a few lines later, to the lower stage herself, bringing, so to speak, her bedroom with her—since this apparently is what she must have done.[7] For neither Senate House, Monument nor balcony had rights and reality of their own. They existed for the convenience of the actors, whose touch gave them life, a shadowy life at most; neglected, they existed no longer.[8]

Shakespeare's stagecraft concentrates, and inevitably, upon opportunity for the actor. We think now of the plays themselves; their first public knew them by their acting; and the development of the actor's art from the agilities and funniments of the clown, and from round-mouthed rhetoric to imaginative interpreting of character by such standards as Hamlet set up for his players, was a factor in the drama's triumph that we now too often ignore. Shakespeare himself, intent more and more upon plucking out the heart of the human mystery, stimulated his actors to a poignancy and intimacy of emotional expression—still can stimulate them to it—as no other playwright has quite learned to do.

## The Speaking of the Verse

His verse was, of course, his chief means to this emotional expression; and when it comes to staging the plays, the speaking of verse must be the foundation of all study. The changes of three hundred years have of themselves put difficulties in our way here; though there are some besides—as one imagines—of Shakespeare's own making. Surely his syntax must now and then have puzzled even his contemporaries. Could they have made much more than we can of Leontes'

> Affection! thy intention stabs the centre;
> Thou dost make possible things not so held,
> Communicat'st with dreams;—How can this be?
> With what's unreal thou coactive art,
> And fellow'st nothing; then, 'tis very credent
> Thou may'st co-join with something; and thou dost;
> And that beyond commission; and I find it,
> And that to the infection of my brains,
> And hardening of my brows.

The confusion of thought and intricacy of language is dramatically justified. Shakespeare is picturing a genuinely jealous man (the sort of man that Othello was *not*) in the grip of a mental epilepsy. We parse the passage and dispute its sense; spoken, as it was meant to be, in a choking torrent of passion, probably a modicum of

effect of it; though the less he does so, perhaps, the better for his play and the more gratitude the better sort of actress will show him. But Shakespeare makes no such demands, has left no blank spaces for her to fill with her charm. He asks instead for self-forgetful clarity of perception, and for a sensitive, spirited, athletic beauty of speech and conduct, which will leave prettiness and its lures at a loss, and the crudities of more Circean appeal looking very crude indeed.

## The Soliloquy

THIS convention of the boy-actress may be said to give a certain remoteness to a play's acting. The soliloquy brings a compensating intimacy, and its use was an important part of Shakespeare's stagecraft. Its recognized usefulness was for the disclosing of the plot, but he soon improved upon this. Soliloquy becomes the means by which he brings us not only to a knowledge of the more secret thoughts of his characters, but into the closest emotional touch with them too. Here the platform stage helped him, as the stage of scenic illusion now defeats his purpose. But it is not altogether a question of 'realism' and the supposed obligation this lays upon a real man in a real-looking room to do nothing he would not do if the whole affair were real.

There is no escape from convention in the theatre, and all conventions can be made acceptable, though they cannot all be used indiscriminately, for they are founded in the physical conditions of the stage of their origin and are often interdependent one with another. Together they form a code, and they are as a treaty made with the audience. No article of it is to be abrogated unless we can be persuaded to consent, and upon its basis we surrender our imaginations to the playwright.

With the soliloquy upon the platform stage it is a case—as so often where convention is concerned—of extremes meeting. There is no illusion, so there is every illusion. Nothing very strange about this man, not even the dress he wears, leaning forward a little we could touch him; we are as intimate and familiar with him as it is possible to be. We agree to call him 'Hamlet', to suppose that he is where he says he is, we admit that he thinks aloud and in blank verse too. It is possible that the more we are asked to imagine the easier we find it to do. It is certain that, once our imagination is working, visual illusion will count for little in the stimulating of emotion beside this intimacy that allows the magnetism of personality full play.

There is no more important task for the producer of Shakespeare than to restore to the soliloquy its rightful place in a play's economy, and in particular to regain for it full emotional effect. We now accept the convention frigidly, the actor manoeuvres with it timidly. Banished behind footlights into that other world of illusion, the solitary self-communing figure rouses our curiosity at best. Yet further adapted to the self-contained methods of modern acting, the soliloquy has quite inevitably become a slack link in the play's action, when it should be a recurring reinforcement to its strength. Shakespeare never pinned so many dramatic fortunes to a merely utilitarian device. Time and again he may be feeling his way through a scene for a grip on his audience, and it is the soliloquy ending it that will give him—and his actor—the stranglehold. When he wishes to quicken the pulse of the action, to screw up its tension in a second or so, the soliloquy serves him well. For a parallel to its full effectiveness on Shakespeare's stage we should really look to the modern music-hall comedian getting on terms with his audience. We may measure the response to Burbage's

O, that this too too solid flesh would melt...

by recalling—those of us that happily can—Dan Leno
as a washerwoman, confiding domestic troubles to a
theatre full of friends, and taken unhindered to their
hearts. The problem is not really a difficult one. If we
solve the physical side of it by restoring, in essentials,
the relation between actor and audience that the intimacy of the platform stage provided, the rest should soon
solve itself.

## Costume

THE problem of costume, when it arises, is a subtler one;
nor probably is it capable of any logical solution. Half
the plays can be quite appropriately dressed in the
costume of Shakespeare's own time. It is a false logic
which suggests that to match their first staging we should
dress them in the costume of ours. For with costume
goes custom and manners—or the lack of them. It may
be both a purge and a tonic to the sluggish-fancied
spectator to be shown a Prince of Denmark in coat and
trousers and a Grave-digger in a bowler hat, for remin-
der that here is a play, not a collection of ritualized
quotations. But physic is for the sick; also, there may be
less drastic cures. When archaeology took hold upon the
nineteenth-century mind it became a matter of moment
to lodge Hamlet in historic surroundings; and withers
were wrung by the anachronisms of ducats and a murder
of Gonzago, French rapiers and the rest. A needlessly
teasing difficulty; why reproduce it in terms of a young
man in a dinner jacket searching for a sword—a thing
not likely to be lying about in his modern mother's sitting
room—with which to kill Polonius, who certainly has
window curtains to hide behind instead of arras? This

gain of intimacy—with a Hamlet we might find sitting opposite at a dinner party—may well be a gain in sympathy. It was originally a great gain, a gift to Shakespeare's audience. But we pay too high a price for it.

What was the actual Elizabethan practice in this matter of costuming is not comprehensively known. We can only say safely that, as with other matters, it was neither constant, consistent, nor, from our present point of view, rational. It was based upon the use of the clothes of the time; but these might be freely and fantastically adapted to suit a particular play or advantage some character in it. Dramatic effect was probably the first consideration and the last. There were such fancy dresses as Oberon or Puck or Caliban might wear; there was always the symbolizing of royalty, and a king would wear a crown whenever he could; there was the utility of knowing Romans from Britons by sight in *Cymbeline*, the martial Roman from the effete Egyptian in *Antony and Cleopatra*, and a Scottish lord when you saw him in *Macbeth*, if we may judge by Malcolm's comment upon Rosse's appearance:

> My countryman; and yet I know him not.

Our difficulty, of course, arises mainly over the historical plays. Not over the English Histories, even so; we can dress Richard III or Henry V by the light of our own superior knowledge of what they wore, and never find it clash violently with anything Shakespeare has put on their backs or in their mouths. But when we come to Julius Cæsar plucking open his doublet, to the conspirators against him with their hats about their ears, and to Cleopatra's

> Cut my lace, Charmian.

not to mention British Imogen in her doublet and hose, we must stop and consider.

The common practice is, in these instances, to ignore the details of Shakespeare's text altogether; to dress Cæsar in his toga, Cleopatra in her habit as she lived, with never a stay-lace about her (though, truly, the costumier, let alone, will tend to get his fashion a few thousand years wrong and turn her out more like the wife of Tutankhamen); and as to Imogen and her surroundings, we do our best to compromise with skins and woad. This may be a lesser evil than presenting a Cæsar recalling Sir Walter Raleigh and a Cleopatra who would make us think of Mary Queen of Scots, but it is no solution of the problem. For the actors have to speak these lines, and if action and appearance contradict them, credibility is destroyed. And the constant credibility of the actor must be a producer's first care. Nor is this all, nor is it, perhaps, the most important thing to consider. The plays are full of reference, direct and indirect, to Elizabethan custom. They are, further, impregnated with what we call 'Renaissance feeling', some more, some less, but all to a degree. Now of this last we have a sense which is likelier to be a better help to their appreciation than any newfangled knowledge of the correct cut of Cleopatra's clothes will be! We know Iago for a Machiavellian figure (so called), and miss none of Shakespeare's intention. But if ever two men breathed the air of a sixteenth-century court, Hamlet and Claudius of Denmark do, and to relate them in habit and behaviour to the twilight figures of Saxo Grammaticus is as much a misinterpretation as any mauling of the text can be. They exist essentially doubtless—as do all the major characters of the plays—in their perennial humanity. But never let us forget the means by which this deeper truth of them is made vivid and actual. There have been better intellects than Shakespeare's, and poetry as good as his. He holds his supreme place by his dramatist's necessary power of bringing thought and vague emotion to the terms of action and convincing speech; further, and far more than is often allowed, by his peculiar gift of bringing into contribution the commonplace traffic of life. However wide the spoken word may range, there must be the actor, anchored to the stage. However high, then, with Shakespeare, the thought or emotion may soar, we shall always find the transcendental set in the familiar. He keeps this balance constantly adjusted; and, at his play's greatest moments, when he must make most sure of our response, he will employ the simplest means. The higher arguments of the plays are thus kept always within range, and their rooted humanity blossoms in a fertile upspringing of expressive little things. Neglect or misinterpret these, the inner wealth of Shakespeare will remain, no doubt, and we may mine for it, but we shall have levelled his landscape bare.

Shakespeare's own attitude in this matter of costume and customs was as inconsistent as his practice was casual. He knew what *his* Cæsar or Cleopatra would be wearing and would casually drop in a reference to it. Yet the great Romans themselves were aliens to him. The great idea of Rome fired his imagination. Brutus, Cassius and Antony do not turn typical Elizabethan gentlemen; and to the end of that play he is striving to translate Plutarch. Whenever, on the other hand, even for a moment he has made a character all his own, he cannot but clothe it in lively familiar detail. Cleopatra's are the coquetries of a great lady of his own time, in their phrasing, in the savour. When the heights of the tragedy have to be scaled, manners will not so much matter. But if we make her, at the play's beginning, a pseudo-classic, languishing Oriental, we must do it in spite of Shakespeare, not by his help. What then is the solution of this problem, if the sight of the serpent of old Nile in a farthingale will too dreadfully offend us? We can compromise. Look at Tintoretto's and Paolo Veronese's paintings of 'classic' subjects. We accept them readily enough.

Sometimes, within the boundaries of a play, the centuries seem all at odds. *Cymbeline* need not trouble us, its Roman Britain is pure 'once upon a time'. But in *King Lear*, for instance, Shakespeare is at unwonted pains to throw us back into some heathen past. Yet Edmund is another Iago, Edgar might have been at Wittenberg with Hamlet, and Oswald steps straight from the seventeenth-century London streets. Here, though, the dominant barbarism is the important thing; the setting for Goneril and Regan, Lear's tyranny and madness, and Gloucester's blinding. To a seventeenth-century audience Oswald was so identifiable a figure that it would not matter greatly how he dressed; the modern designer of costume must show him up as best he may. Each play, in fine, if it presents a problem at all, presents its own.

## The Integrity of the Text

THE text, one says at first blush, can present no problem at all. The plays should be acted as Shakespeare wrote them—how dispute it? They should be; and it is as well, before we discuss hard cases, to have the principle freely admitted. Lip service enough is done it nowadays, and Colley Cibber's *Richard III*, Tate's *Lear* and Garrick's improvements are at the back of our bookshelves, but we still find Messrs John Doe and Richard Roe slicing out lines by the dozen and even a scene or so, or chopping and changing them to suit their scenery. This will not do. Shakespeare was not a perfect playwright; there can be no such thing. Nor did he aim at a mechanical perfection, but a vitality, and this he achieved. At best then, we cut and carve the body of a play to its peril. It may be robustly, but it may be very delicately organized. And we still know little enough of the laws of its existence, and some of us, perhaps, are not such very skilful surgeons; nor is any surgeon to be recommended who operates for his own convenience.

This good rule laid down, what are the exceptions that go to prove it? There is the pornographic difficulty. This is not such a stumbling block to us as it was to Bowdler, to some bright young eyes nowadays it is quite imperceptible, in fact. Yet, saving their presence, it exists; for it exists aesthetically. Shakespeare's characters often make obscene jokes. The manners of his time permitted it. The public manners of ours still do not. Now the dramatic value of a joke is to be measured by its effect upon an audience, and each is meant to make its own sort of effect. If then, instead of giving them a passing moment's amusement, it makes a thousand people uncomfortable and for the next five minutes very self-conscious, it fails of its true effect. This argument must not be stretched to cover the silliness of turning 'God' into 'Heaven' and of making Othello call Desdemona a 'wanton' (the practice, as I recollect, of the eighteen-nineties), nor to such deodorizing of *Measure for Measure* that it becomes hard to discover what all the fuss is about. If an audience cannot think of Angelo and the Duke, Pompey and Lucio, Isabella and Mistress Overdone, and themselves to boot, as fellow-creatures all, the play is not for them. Othello must call Desdemona a 'whore', and let those that do not like it leave the theatre; what have such queasy minds to do with the pity and terror of her murder and his death? Again, to make Beatrice so mealymouthed that she may not tell us how the devil is to meet her at the gates of hell, 'like an old cuckold with horns on his head', is to dress her in a crinoline, not a farthingale. But suppression of a few of the more scabrous jokes will not leave a play much the poorer; nor, one may add, will the average playgoer be much the wiser or merrier for hearing them, since they are often quite hard to understand.

Topical passages are a similar difficulty. With their savour, if not their very meaning lost, they show like dead wood in the living tree of the dialogue and are better, one would suppose, cut away. But no hard and fast rule will apply. Macbeth's porter's farmer and equivocator will never win spontaneous laughter again. But we cannot away with them, or nothing is left of the porter. Still the baffled low comedian must not, as his wont is, obscure the lines with bibulous antics. There will be that little dead spot in the play, and nothing can be done about it. Rosencrantz' reference to the 'eyrie of children' is meaningless except to the student. Is the play the poorer for the loss of it? But the logic that will take this out had better not rob us of

> Dead shepherd, now I find thy saw of might;
> Who ever loved that loved not at first sight?

And there is the strange case of

The lady of the Strachy married the yeoman of the wardrobe.

Nobody knows what it means, but everybody finds it funny when it is spoken in its place. And this has its parallels.

In general, however, better play the plays as we find them. The blue pencil is a dangerous weapon; and its use grows on a man, for it solves too many little difficulties far too easily.

Lastly, for a golden rule, whether staging or costuming or cutting is in question, and a comprehensive creed, a producer might well pin this on his wall: Gain Shakespeare's effects by Shakespeare's means when you can; for, plainly, this will be the better way. But gain Shakespeare's effects; and it is your business to discern them.

1927

## Notes

1   But it should not be forgotten that Sir Herbert Tree, happy in the orthodoxy of public favour, welcomed the heretic Mr Poel more than once to a share in his Shakespeare Festivals.

2   I do not deal in general therefore with certain vexed questions, such as act-division, which still need to be looked at, I think, in the light of the particular play.

3   I remember a most intelligent reader of a modern play missing the whole point of a scene through which the chief character was to sit conspicuously and eloquently silent. He counted only with the written dialogue. I remember, when I thought I knew *King Lear* well enough, being amazed at the effect, all dialogue apart, of the mere meeting, when I saw it, of blind Gloucester and mad Lear.

4   Though, in a sense, there was no first performance of *Hamlet*. And doubtless many of the audience for Shakespeare's new version of the old play only thought he had spoiled a good story of murder and revenge by adding too much talk to it.

5   Unless it may be said that we learn in the scene after whereabouts he *was*.

6   And in *Coriolanus*, which probably postdates *Antony and Cleopatra*, with Marcius' 'A goodly city is this Antium,' we are back to the barely informative. It serves Shakespeare's purpose; he asks no more.

7   I fancy, though, that the later Shakespeare would have thought this a clumsy device.

8   How far this is true of other dramatists than Shakespeare I do not pretend to say; nor how far, with him, the influence of the private theatre, making undoubtedly towards the scenic stage

and (much later) for illusion, did not modify his practice, when he had that stage to consider. A question, again, for the bibliographers and historians.

9  There is no evidence, of course, that he felt it a loss, no such reference to the insufficiency of the boy-actress as there is to the overself-sufficiency of the clown. Women did appear in the Masques, if only to dance, so the gulf to be bridged was not a broad one. But the Elizabethan was as shocked by the notion of women appearing upon the public stage as the Chinese playgoer is today.

# The Merchant of Venice

THE MERCHANT OF VENICE is a fairy tale. There is no more reality in Shylock's bond and the Lord of Belmont's will than in Jack and the Beanstalk.

Shakespeare, it is true, did not leave the fables as he found them. This would not have done; things that pass muster on the printed page may become quite incredible when acted by human beings, and the unlikelier the story, the likelier must the mechanism of its acting be made. Besides, when his own creative impulse was quickened, he could not help giving life to a character; he could no more help it than the sun can help shining. So Shylock is real, while his story remains fabulous; and Portia and Bassanio become human, though, truly, they never quite emerge from the enchanted thicket of fancy into the common light of day. Aesthetic logic may demand that a story and its characters should move consistently upon one plane or another, be it fantastic or real. But Shakespeare's practical business, once he had chosen these two stories for his play, was simply so to charge them with humanity that they did not betray belief in the human beings presenting them, yet not so uncompromisingly that the stories themselves became ridiculous.

What the producer of the play must first set himself to ascertain is the way in which he did this, the nice course that—by reason or instinct—he steered. Find it and follow it, and there need be no running on the rocks. But logic may land us anywhere. It can turn Bassanio into a heartless adventurer. Test the clock of the action by Greenwich time, it will either be going too fast or too slow. And as to Portia's disguise and Bellario's law, would the village policeman be taken in by either? But the actor will find that he simply cannot play Bassanio as a humbug, for Shakespeare does not mean him to. Portias and Nerissas have been eclipsed by wigs and spectacles. This is senseless tomfoolery; but how make a wiseacre producer see that if he does not already know? And if, while Shylock stands with his knife ready and Antonio with his bared breast, the wise young judge lifting a magical finger between them, we sit questioning Bellario's law—why, no one concerned, actors or audience, is for this fairyland, that is clear.

*The Merchant of Venice* is the simplest of plays, so long as we do not bedevil it with sophistries. Further, it is—for what it is!—as smoothly and completely successful, its means being as well fitted to its end, as anything Shakespeare wrote. He was happy in his choice of the Portia story; his verse, which has lost glitter to gain a mellower beauty and an easier flow, is now well attuned to such romance. The story of Shylock's bond is good contrast and complement both; and he can now project character upon the stage, uncompromising and complete. Yet this Shylock does not overwhelm the play, as at a later birth he might well have done—it is a near thing, though! Lastly, Shakespeare is now enough of the skilled playwright to be able to adjust and blend the two themes with fruitful economy.

## The Construction of the Play

### THE PROBLEM OF 'DOUBLE TIME'

THIS blending of the themes would, to a modern playwright, have been the main difficulty. The two stories do not naturally march together. The forfeiture of the bond must be a matter of months; with time not only of the essence of the contract, but of the dramatic effect. But the tale of the caskets cannot be enlarged, its substance is too fragile; and a very moderate charge of emotion would explode its pretty hollowness altogether. Critics have credited Shakespeare with nice calculation and amazing subtlety in his compassing of the time-difficulty. Daniel gives us one analysis, Halpin another, Eccles a third, and Furness finds the play as good a peg for the famous Double Time theory as Wilson, its inventor, found *Othello*. All very ingenious; but is the ingenuity Shakespeare's or their own?[1] For him dramatic time was a naturally elastic affair. (It still is, though less so, for the modern playwright, whose half-hour act may commonly suggest the passing of an hour or two; this also is Double Time.) Shakespeare seems to think of it quite simply in terms of effect, as he thought of dramatic space, moving his characters hither and thither without considering the compassing of yards or miles. The one freedom will imply and enhance the other. The dramatist working for the 'realistic' stage must settle definitely where his characters are to be and keep them there till he chooses to change the scenery. Shakespeare need not; and, in fact, he never insists upon place at all, unless it suits him to; and then only to the extent that suits him.[2] In this play, for instance, where we find Shylock and Antonio will be Venice, but whereabouts in Venice is usually no matter; when it is—at Shylock's door or in court before the Duke—it will be made clear enough to us. And where Portia is, is Belmont. He treats time—and the more easily—with a like freedom, and a like aim. Three months suits for the bond; but once he has pouched the money Bassanio must be off to Belmont, and his calendar, attuned to his mood, at once starts to run by hours only. The wind serves, and he sails that very night, and there is no delay at Belmont. Portia

would detain him some month or two before he ventures;
and what could be more convenient for a Shakespeare
bent on synchronizing the two stories? For that matter,
he could have placed Belmont a few hundred miles off,
and let the coming and going eke out the time. Did the
problem as a whole ever even occur to him? If it did,
he dismissed it as of no consequence. What he does is
to set each story going according to its nature; then he
punctuates them, so to speak, for effect. By the clock
they are not even consistent in themselves, far less with
each other. But we should pay just the sort of attention
to these months, days or hours that we do, in another
connection, to the commas and semicolons elucidating
a sentence. They give us, and are meant to, simply a
*sense* of time and its exactions. It is the more easily done
because our own sense of time in daily life is far from
consistent. Time flies when we are happy, and drags in
anxiety, as poets never tire of reminding us. Shakespeare's own reflections on the phenomenon run to half
a column of the concordance, and he turns it quite
naturally to dramatic account.

## THE TRUE PROBLEM

How to blend two such disparate themes into a dramatically organic whole; that was his real problem. The
stories, linked in the first scene, will, of themselves, soon
part company. Shakespeare has to run them neck and
neck till he is ready to join them again in the scene of
the trial. But the difficulty is less that they will not match
each other by the clock than that their whole gait so
differs, their very nature. How is the flimsy theme of the
caskets to be kept in countenance beside its grimly
powerful rival? You cannot, as we said, elaborate the story,
or charge it with emotion; that would invite disaster.

Imagine a Portia seriously alarmed by the prospect of an Aragon or a Morocco for husband. What sort of barrier, on the other hand, would the caskets be to a flesh-and-blood hero and heroine fallen in love? Would a Romeo or Rosalind give a snap of the finger for them? As it is, the very sight of Bassanio prompts Portia to rebellion; and Shakespeare can only allow his lovers a few lines of talk together, and that in company, dare only colour the fairy tale with a rhetorically passionate phrase or so before the choice is made and the caskets can be forgotten—as they are!—altogether. Nor does anything in the play show the artist's supreme tact in knowing what *not* to do better than this?

But you cannot neglect the Portia story either, or our interest in her may cool. Besides, this antiphony of high romance and rasping hate enhances the effect of both. A contrasting of subjects, scene by scene, is a trick (in no depreciatory sense) of Shakespeare's earliest stage-craft, and he never lost his liking for it.[3] Then if the casket-theme cannot be neglected, but cannot be elaborated, it must somehow be drawn out, its peculiar character sustained, its interest husbanded while its consummation is delayed.

Shakespeare goes straightforwardly enough to work. He puts just as little as may be into Portia's first scene; but for the one sounding of Bassanio's name there would be only the inevitable tale of the caskets told in tripping prose and the conventional joking upon the suitors. Portia and Nerissa, however, seen for the first time in the flesh, give it sufficient life, and that 'Bassanio' one vivid spark more. Later, in due course, come Morocco's choice of the gold casket and Aragon's of the silver. We remark that Morocco is allotted two scenes instead of one. The reason is, probably, that Shakespeare has now enriched himself with the Lorenzo-Jessica story (not to mention the episode of the Gobbos, father and son), and, with this extra weight in the Venetian scale of the action, is put to it to maintain the balance. He could, of course, finish with both Morocco and Aragon earlier and give Bassanio two scenes instead of one.[4] And if a romantic hero could not well wait till after dinner to make his choice, as Morocco does, Solanio's arrival with the ill news of Antonio could easily have been kept for the later scene. But this will not do either—most characteristically will not do for Shakespeare. He has held his lovers apart, since the air of the Belmont of the caskets is too rarefied for flesh and blood to breathe. And Portia herself has been spellbound; we have only had jaunty little Nerissa to prophesy that love (by the pious prevision of the late lord) would somehow find out the way.[5] But once he brings them together Bassanio must break the spell. It is the story of the sleeping beauty and the prince in another kind; a legitimate and traditional outcome. And once Shakespeare himself has broken free of the fairy tale and brought these two to life (for Bassanio as well has been till now a little bloodless) it is not in him to let them lapse from the scene unproved, and to the full. The long restraint has left him impatient, and he must, here and now, have his dramatic fling. We need not credit—or discredit him, if you like—with much calculation of the problem. It was common prudence both to keep Belmont as constantly in our view as Venice, and the emancipating Bassanio clear of it for as long as possible. And he is now in the middle of his play, rather past it, ready to link his two stories together again. He worked forthrightly; that is written plain over most of his work. Though he might now find that he had here material for two scenes, he would not return in his tracks, telescope Aragon and Morocco—and take, in fact, all the sort of trouble we, who are his critics, must take to explain what a much more compact job he could have made of it! Besides, here is his chance to uplift the two as hero and heroine, and he will not dissipate its effectiveness.

For Bassanio, as we said, has been till now only little less bound than Portia in the fetters of a fairy tale; and later, Shylock and the bond will condemn him to protesting helplessness, and the affair of the rings to be merrily befooled.[6] The wonder indeed is, considering the rather poor figure—painfully poor by the gospel according to Samuel Smiles—the coercion of the story makes him cut, that throughout he measures up so well to the stature of sympathetic hero. Shakespeare contrives it in two ways. He endows him with very noble verse; and, whenever he can, throws into strong relief the Bassanio of his own uncovenanted imagination. He does this here. The fantasy of the caskets brought to its due crisis, charged with an emotion which blows it for a finish into thin air, he shows us Bassanio, his heart's desire won, agonized with grief and remorse at the news of Antonio's danger. Such moments do test a man and show him for what he is; and this one, set in bright light and made the scene's turning point, counts for more in the effect the character makes on us than all the gentlemanly graces of his conventional equipment. Unless the actor is much at fault, we shall hear the keynote to the true Bassanio struck in the quiet simplicity—such contrast to his rhetoric over the caskets, even though this was less mere rhetoric than Morocco's and Aragon's—of the speech which begins

> O sweet Portia,
> Here are a few of the unpleasant'st words
> That ever blotted paper! . . .
> Rating myself at nothing, you shall see

> How much I was a braggart. When I told you
> My state was nothing, I should then have told you
> That I was worse than nothing; for indeed
> I have engaged myself to a dear friend,
> Engaged my friend to his mere enemy,
> To feed my means. . . .

Here speaks Shakespeare's Bassanio; and it is by this, and all that will belong to it, that he is meant to live in our minds.

Producer and actors must look carefully into the way by which in this scene the method that has served for the casket story is resolved into something better fitted to the theme of the bond (dominant from the beginning of the play, and now to absorb and transform the dedicated Portia and her fortunes). It is a change—though we must not insist on the contrast more than Shakespeare does—from dramatic convention to dramatic life. From the beginning the pulse of the scene beats more strongly; and Portia's

> I pray you, tarry: pause a day or two
> Before you hazard; for in choosing wrong,
> I lose your company; therefore forbear awhile. . . .

is not only deeper in feeling (there has been little or nothing to rouse her till now; she has had to be the picture of a Portia, hardly more, with a spice of wit to help her through), but how much simpler in expression! When Bassanio turns to those obsessing caskets she must lapse again for a space into fancies of his swanlike end, her eye the watery deathbed for him, into talk about Hercules and Alcides (borrowed, one fears, from Morocco), about Dardanian wives and the like—even as he will be conventionally sententious over his choice. But note how, within the convention, preparing an escape from it, emotion is roused and sustained. With the rhetoric of Portia's

> Go, Hercules!
> Live thou, I live: with much, much more dismay
> I view the fight, than thou that mak'st the fray.

for a springboard, the song and its music are to stir us,

> *whilst Bassanio comments on the caskets to himself.*

So (let the actor remember) when he does at last speak, the emotional ascent will have been half climbed for him already. And while he pays his tribute of trope and maxim, Portia, Nerissa and the rest watch him in silence, at full strain of attention, and help to keep us, too, intent. The speech itself sweeps unhindered to its height, and the pause while the casket is unlocked is filled and enriched by the intensity of Portia's

> How all the other passions fleet to air . . .

most cunningly contrived in meaning and melody, with its emphasis on 'despair' and 'ecstasy' and 'excess', to hold us upwrought. The fairy tale is finally incarnate in the fantastic word-painting of the portrait and the reading of the scroll. Then, with a most delicate declension to reality, Bassanio comes to face her as in a more actual world, and the curtains can be drawn upon the caskets for the last time. Observe that not for a moment has Shakespeare played his fabulous story false. He takes his theatre too seriously to go spoiling an illusion he has created. He consummates it, and turns the figures of it to fresh purpose, and they seem to suffer no change.

Throughout the scene—throughout the play, and the larger part of all Elizabethan drama for that matter— effects must be valued very much in terms of music. And, with the far adventuring of his playwriting hardly

begun, Shakespeare's verse is already fairly flawless, and
its manoeuvring from mood to mood masterly, if still
simple. We have the royal humility of the speech in
which Portia yields herself (Bassanio slips back to his
metaphors for a moment after this); then, for contrast,
the little interlude of Gratiano and Nerissa, with the
tripping monosyllables of Gratiano's

> I wish you all the joy that you can wish;
> For I am sure you can wish none from me. . . .

to mark the pace and the tone of it. Then follows the
arrival of Antonio's messenger with Lorenzo and Jessica;
done in plain, easy-moving verse that will not discount
the distressed silence in which he reads the letter, nor
the quiet candour of his confession to Portia. Now comes
another crescendo—two voices added to strengthen it—
leading up to her generous, wide-eyed

> What sum owes he the Jew?
> BASSANIO. For me, three thousand ducats.
> PORTIA.                     What, no more!
> Pay him six thousand, and deface the bond;
> Double six thousand, and then treble that. . . .

which itself drops to the gentleness of

> Since you are dear bought I will love you dear.

Then, to strengthen the scene's ending, we have the
austere prose of Antonio's letter, chilling us to misgiving.
And since—in stage practice, and with the prevailing key
of the play's writing to consider—this will not do for an
actual finish, there is a last modulation into the brisk
coda of

> Since I have your good leave to go away,
> I will make haste: but till I come again,

No bed shall e'er be guilty of my stay,
Nor rest be interposer 'twixt us twain.

Lorenzo and Jessica make another link (though their relation to Belmont is pretty arbitrary) between the two stories. This, however, is but the secondary use of them. There must be a sense of time passing in Venice while the bond matures, yet we must have continuous action there, too, while the ritual at Belmont goes its measured way; so, as there can be little for Shylock and Antonio to do but wait, this third, minor theme is interposed. It brings fresh impetus to the action as well as new matter; and it shows us—very usefully—another and more human side of Shylock. Shakespeare does not scheme it out overcarefully. The masking and the elopement and the coming and going they involve are rather inconveniently crowded together (the pleasant episode of the Gobbos may have stolen a little necessary space); and one chapter of the story—for were we perhaps to have seen Shylock at supper with Bassanio, Lorenzo and the rest while the disguised Jessica waited on them?—was possibly crowded out altogether.

Once the fugitives, with some disregard of likelihood, have been brought to Belmont, Gobbo in attendance, Shakespeare turns them to account quite shamelessly. They play a mighty poor scene to give Portia and Nerissa time to disguise themselves as doctor and clerk.[7] They will have to play another while doctor and clerk change to Portia and Nerissa again; but for that, as if in compensation, they are to be dowered with the loveliest lines in the play.[8] With the junction of the themes in the trial-scene the constructive problem is, of course, solved. Shylock disappearing, the rest is simple.

# Shakespeare's Venice

IF Lorenzo and Jessica and a little poetry and the consort of music, which no well-regulated great household of his time would be without, are Shakespeare's resources (he had no other; and what better should we ask?) for the painting of the starlit garden of Belmont at the play's end, for its beginning he must show us Venice. He troubles with no verbal scene-painting here; throughout the first scene the very word is but spoken twice, and quite casually. We might be anywhere in the city, or out of it, even. Thereafter we hear of the Rialto, of a gondola, of the common ferry and suchlike incidentals; but of the picturesque environment to which modern staging has accustomed us there is no suggestion at all. Yet he does present a Venice that lived in the Elizabethan mind, and it is the Venice of his dramatic needs; a city of royal merchants trading to the gorgeous East, of Jews in their gaberdines (as rare a sight, remember, as to us a Chinese mandarin is, walking the London streets today), and of splendid gentlemen rustling in silks. To the lucky young Englishman who could hope to travel there Venice stood for culture and manners and the luxury of civilization; and this—without one word of description—is how Shakespeare pictures it.

We are used nowadays to see the play begun by the entry of a depressed, sober-suited, middle-aged man and two skipping youths, who make their way with a sort of desperate merriment through such lines as the producer's blue pencil has left them, vanish shamefacedly, reappear at intervals to speak the remnant of another speech or two, and slip at last unregarded into oblivion. These are Solanio and Salarino, cursed by actors as the two worst bores in the whole Shakespearean canon; not excepting, even, those other twin brethren in nonentity, Rosencrantz and Guildenstern.[9] As characters, Shakespeare has certainly not been at much pains with them; they could exchange speeches and no one would be the wiser, and they move about at everybody's convenience but their own. But they have their use, and it is an important one; realize it, and there may be some credit in fulfilling it. They are there to paint Venice for us, the Venice of the magnificent young man. Bassanio embodies it also; but there are other calls on him, and he will be off to Belmont soon. So do Gratiano and Lorenzo; but they will be gone too. Solanio and Salarino will not fail us; they hoist this flag at the play's beginning and keep it bravely flying for as long as need be. When Salarino, for a beginning, addresses Antonio with

> There, where your argosies with portly sail,
> Like signiors and rich burghers on the flood,
> Or, as it were, the pageants of the sea,
> Do overpeer the petty traffickers,
> That curt'sy to them, do them reverence
> As they fly by them with their woven wings.

—there should be no skipping merriment in this.

They are argosies themselves, these magnificent young men, of high-flowing speech; pageants to overpeer the callow English ruffians, to whom they are here displayed. The talk passes from spices and silks into fine classical phrases; and with what elaborate, dignified dandyism it ends!

*Enter Bassanio, Lorenzo and Gratiano.*

SOLANIO. Here comes Bassanio, your most noble kinsman,
  Gratiano, and Lorenzo. Fare you well;
  We leave you now with better company.
SALARINO. I would have stayed till I had made you merry,
  If worthier friends had not prevented me.

ANTONIO. Your worth is very dear in my regard.
  I take it, your own business calls on you,
And you embrace the occasion to depart.
SALARINO. Good-morrow, my good lords.
BASSANIO. Good signiors both, when shall we laugh? Say,
  when?
  You grow exceeding strange: Must it be so?
SALARINO. We'll make our leisures to attend on yours.

No apologetic gabbling here: but such a polish, polish
as might have satisfied Mr Turveydrop. Solanio—if one
could distinguish between them—might cut the finer
figure of the two. When the Masque is in question:

> 'Tis vile [he says], unless it may be quaintly ordered,
> And better, in my mind, not undertook.

Salarino has a cultured young gentleman's turn for
classical allusion. He ranges happily from two-headed
Janus and Nestor to Venus' pigeons.
  But it is, as we said, when Bassanio and Gratiano and
Lorenzo with his Jessica have departed, that the use
these two are to the play becomes plainest. They give
us the first news of Antonio's losses, and hearsay, filtering
through them, keeps the disaster conveniently vague. If
we saw the blow fall on Antonio, the far more dramatic
scene in which Shylock is thrown from depth to heights
and from heights to depth as ill news and this good news
strike upon him would be left at a discount. In this scene
they are most useful (if they are not made mere targets
for a star actor to shoot at). For here again is Venice,
in the contrast between sordid Shylock and Tubal and
our magnificent young gentlemen, superfine still of
speech and manner, but not above a little Jew-baiting.
They sustain that theme—and it must be sustained—till
it can be fully and finally orchestrated in the trial-scene.

It is a simple stagecraft which thus employs them, and their vacuity as characters inclines us to forget this, their very real utility. Forgetting it, Shakespeare's histrionic Venice is too often forgotten also.

## The Characters,
## and the Crisis of the Action

NONE of the minor characters does much more than illustrate the story; at best, they illuminate with a little lively detail their own passage through it. Not the Duke, nor Morocco, Aragon, Tubal, Lorenzo, Jessica, nor the Gobbos, nor Nerissa, had much being in Shakespeare's mind, we feel, apart from the scenes they played, and the use they were to him. It is as futile, that is to say, to discuss Jessica's excuses for gilding herself with ducats when she elopes as it is to work out her itinerary via Genoa to Belmont; we might as well start writing the life-story of Mistress Margery Gobbo.

### PORTIA

Shakespeare can do little enough with Portia while she is still the slave of the caskets; incidentally, the actress must resist the temptation to try and do more. She has this picture of an enchanted princess to present, verse and prose to speak perfectly, and she had better be content with that. But we feel, nevertheless (and in this, very discreetly, she may at once encourage us), that here, pent up and primed for escape, is one of that eminent succession of candid and fearless souls: Rosaline, Helena, Beatrice, Rosalind—they embodied an ideal lodged for long in Shakespeare's imagination; he gave it expression whenever he could. Once he can set his Portia free to

be herself, he quickly makes up for lost time. He has
need to; for from the moment of that revealing

> You see me, Lord Bassanio, where I stand. . . .

not half the play's life is left her, and during a good part
of this she must pose as the young doctor of Rome whose
name is Balthasar. He does not very deliberately develop
her character; he seems by now to know too much about
her to need to do that. He reveals it to us mainly in
little things, and lets us feel its whole happy virtue in
the melody of her speech. This it is that casts its spell
upon the strict court of Venice. The

> Shed thou no blood. . . .

is an effective trick. But

> The quality of mercy is not strained;
> It droppeth as the gentle rain from heaven
> Upon the place beneath. . . .

with its continuing beauty, gives the true Portia. To the
very end she expands in her fine freedom, growing in
authority and dignity, fresh touches of humour enlight-
ening her, new traits of graciousness showing. She is a
great lady in her perfect simplicity, in her ready tact (see
how she keeps her guest Antonio free from the mock
quarrel about the rings), and in her quite unconscious
self-sufficiency (she jokes without embarrassment about
taking the mythical Balthasar to her bed, but she snubs
Gratiano the next minute for talking of cuckoldry, even
as she snubbed Nerissa for a very mild indelicacy—she
is fond of Nerissa, but no forward waiting-women for
her!). Yet she is no more than a girl.

Here is an effect that we are always apt to miss in the
acting of Shakespeare today. It is not the actress's fault
that she cannot be what her predecessor, the boy-Portia,

was; and she brings us compensation for losses which should leave us—if she will mitigate the losses as far as she can—gainers on the whole. But the constant play made in the Comedies upon the contrast between womanly passion or wisdom and its very virginal enshrining gives a delicacy and humour to these figures of romance which the limited resources of the boy left vivid, which the ampler endowment of the woman too often obscures. This is no paradox, but the obvious result of a practical artistry making the most of its materials. Portia does not abide in this dichotomy as fully as, for instance, Rosalind and Viola do; but Shakespeare turns it to account with her in half a hundred little ways, and to blur the effect of them is to rob her of much distinction.

The very first line she speaks, the

> By my troth, Nerissa, my little body is aweary of this great world.

is likely to come from the mature actress robbed of half its point. This will not matter so much. But couple that 'little body' with her self-surrender to Bassanio as

> an unlessoned girl, unschooled, unpractised;
> Happy in this, she is not yet so old
> But she may learn. . . .

and with the mischief that hides behind the formal courtesies of the welcome to Aragon and Morocco, with the innocence of the amazed

> What no more!
> Pay him six thousand and deface the bond. . . .

with the pretty sententiousness of her talk of herself, her

> I never did repent of doing good,
> Nor shall not now. . . .

followed by the artless

> This comes too near the praising of myself. . . .

and the figure built up for us of the heiress and great lady of Belmont is seen to be a mere child, too, who lives remote in her enchanted world. Set beside this the Portia of resource and command, who sends Bassanio posthaste to his friend, and beside that the schoolgirl laughing with Nerissa over the trick they are to play their new lords and masters. Know them all for one Portia, a wise and gallant spirit so virginally enshrined; and we see to what profit Shakespeare turned his disabilities. There is, in this play, a twofold artistry in the achievement. Unlikelihood of plot is redeemed by veracity of character; while the artifice of the medium, the verse and its convention, and the stylized acting of boy as woman, re-reconciles us to the fantasy of the plot.

But a boy-Portia's advantage was chiefly manifest, of course, in the scene of the trial; and here in particular the actress of today must see that she lessens it no more than she need. The curious process of what we may call the 'double negative', by which an Elizabethan audience first admitted a boy as a girl and then enjoyed the pretence that the girl was a boy, is obsolete for us; make-believe being the game, there was probably some pleasure just in this complication of it. This beside, there was the direct dramatic effect, which the boy made supremely well in his own person, of the wise young judge, the Daniel come to judgment. Shylock (and Shakespeare) plucks the allusion from the popular story of Susanna; but there may be some happy confusion, perhaps, with that other Daniel who was among ' . . . the children of Israel, of the king's seede and of the Prince's: Springaldes without any blemish, but well-favoured, studious in all wisdome, skillful for knowledge, able to utter knowledge, and such as have livelinesse in them, that they might stand in the king's palace. . . . ' For this is the very figure we should see. Here is the strict court of Venice, like enough to any law court, from East to West, from Shakespeare's time to now, in that it will seem to the stranger there very dry and discouraging, airless, lifeless. Age and incredulity preside; and if passion and life do enter, they must play upon muted strings. The fiercely passionate Shylock is anomaly enough in such surroundings. Then comes this youth, as brisk and businesslike as you please, and stands before the judges' bench, alert, athletic, modest, confident. He is life incarnate and destined to victory; and such a victory is the fitting climax to a fairy tale. So the Portia that will—as most Portias do—lapse into feminine softness and pitch the whole scene in the key of the speech on mercy, and that in a key of sentiment, damns the scene and herself and the speech, all three. This amazing youth has the ear of the court at once; but he'll only hold it by strict attention to business. Then, suddenly, out of this, comes the famous appeal, and catches us and the court unaware, catches us by the throat, enkindles us. In this lies the effect. Prepare for it, or make the beauty of it overbeautiful (all the more now, because it is famous and hackneyed) and it becomes a dose of soothing syrup.

This, be it further remembered, is not the scene's top note; conflict and crisis are to come. They are brought about simply and directly; the mechanical trick of the 'No jot of blood' that is to resolve them asks nothing else. Shakespeare keeps the medium of the verse as simple; it flows on with hardly a broken line. The conflict is between Portia and Shylock. Bassanio's agony, Antonio's stoic resignation cannot be given great play; the artifice of the story will not even now sustain crosscurrents of human passion. But the constraint of the business of a court accounts well enough for their quiescence (the actors need do nothing to discount it) and the few notes that are struck from them suffice. The action must sweep ahead and no chance be given us to question its likelihood. Even when all is over the Duke departs with not much more comment upon this amazing case than an invitation to the learned young doctor to come to dinner, and Antonio and his friends are as casual about it and almost as calm. There is tactful skill in this. Shylock has gone, that fairy tale is done with; the less we look back upon it, the sooner we come to fresh comedy again the better.

Throughout the scene a Portia must, of course, by no smallest sign betray to us—as well betray it to Bassanio—that she is other than she now seems. No difficulty here, as we said, for Shakespeare's Portia, or his audience either. There was no wondering as he faced the judges why they never saw this was a woman (since very obviously he now wasn't) nor why Bassanio did not know his wife a yard off. The liquid sentences of the Mercy speech were no betrayal, nor did the brusque aside of a young lawyer, intent upon his brief—

> Your wife would give you little thanks for that,
> If she were by to hear you make the offer.

—lose its quite casual humour. All this straightforwardness the modern actress must, as far as she can, restore.


## ANTONIO, GRATIANO AND OTHERS

In these early plays character does not as a rule outrun the requirements of the plot. Shakespeare is content enough with the decorative, the sententious, the rhetorical, in his casual Venetians, in Aragon and Morocco; with the conventional in Launcelot, who is the stage clown—the juggler with words, neat, agile, resourceful and occasionally familiar with the audience, as a clown and a juggler should be—under a thin disguise of character; with old Gobbo for a minute or two's incidental fun; with the pure utility of Tubal.

Antonio is flesh and blood. He is the passive figure of the story's demand; but Shakespeare refines this in the selflessness that can send Bassanio to Belmont and be happy in a friend's happiness, in the indifference to life that lets him oppose patience to his enemy's fury; and he makes him more convincingly this sort of man by making him just a little self-conscious too.

> In sooth, I know not why I am so sad. . . .

If he does not, it is not for want of thinking about it. He takes a sad pleasure in saying that he is

> a tainted wether of the flock,
> Meetest for death . . .

But there is a redeeming ironic humour in

> You cannot better be employed, Bassanio,
> Then to live still and write mine epitaph.

He is sufficiently set forth, and there is conveyed in him a better dignity than mere words give.[10]

Nerissa is echoing merriment; not much more.

Shakespeare may have had half a mind to make something a little out of the way of Gratiano. He starts him with a temperament and a witty speech; but by the play's end we have not had much more from him than the 'infinite deal of nothing' of Bassanio's gibe, rattling stuff, bouncing the play along, but revealing no latent Gratiano. It all makes a good enough pattern of this sort of man, who will be a useful foil to Bassanio, and can be paired off for symmetry with Portia's foil, Nerissa;

and the play needed no more. But there is enough of
him, and enough talk about him, for one to feel that he
missed by only a little the touch of magic that would
have made something more of him and added him to
the list of those that survive the lowering of the lights
and the theatre's emptying. There is a moment while he
waits to take his share in Jessica's abduction, and sits
reflecting:

> All things that are,
> Are with more spirit chased than enjoyed.
> How like a yonker or a prodigal,
> The scarfed bark puts from her native bay,
> Hugg'd and embraced by the strumpet wind!
> How like a prodigal doth she return;
> With over-weather'd ribs, and ragged sails,
> Torn, rent and beggared by the strumpet wind!

Harsh enough similes for such an occasion! Is this another
side to the agreeable rattle? Does the man who exclaims

> Let me play the fool!
> With mirth and laughter let old wrinkles come. . . .

find life in fact rather bitter to his taste? But one must
beware of reading subtleties into Shakespeare. If such a
Gratiano was ever shadowed in his mind, he made no
solid substance of him.

Bassanio we have spoken of; play the part straightforwardly and it will come right.


## SHYLOCK

There remains Shylock. He steps into the play, actual
and individual from his first word on, and well might in
his strength (we come to feel) have broken the pinchbeck
of his origin to bits, had a later Shakespeare had the

handling of him. As it is, his actuality is not weakened by the fantasy of the bond, as is Portia's by her caskets. For one thing, our credulity is not strained till the time comes for its maturing, and by then—if ever—the play and its acting will have captured us. For another, the law and its ways are normally so uncanny to a layman that the strict court of an exotic Venice might give even stranger judgments than this and only confirm us in our belief that once litigation begins almost anything may happen. Despite the borrowed story, this Shylock is essentially Shakespeare's own. But if he is not a puppet, neither is he a stalking-horse; he is no more a mere means to exemplifying the Semitic problem than is Othello to the raising of the colour question. 'I am a Jew.' 'Haply, for I am black. . . . ' Here we have—and in Shylock's case far more acutely and completely—the *circumstances* of the dramatic conflict; but at the heart of it are men; and we may surmise, indeed, that from a maturer Shakespeare we should have had, as with Othello, much more of the man, and so rather less of the alien and his griefs. However that may be, he steps now into the play, individual and imaginatively full-grown, and the scene of his talk with Bassanio and Antonio is masterly exposition.

The dry taciturnity of his

> Three thousand ducats; well?

(the lure of that thrice-echoed 'Well'!) and the cold dissecting of the business in hand are made colder, drier yet by contrast with the happy sound of Portia's laughter dying in our ears as he begins to speak. And for what a helpless innocent Bassanio shows beside him; over-anxious, touchy, overcivil! Shylock takes his time; and suddenly we see him peering, myopic, beneath his brows. Who can the newcomer be? And the quick brain answers beneath the question's cover: They must need the money badly if Antonio himself comes seeking me. Off goes Bassanio to greet his friend; and Shylock in a long aside can discharge his obligations to the plot." These eleven lines are worth comment. In them is all the motive power for drama that the story, as Shakespeare found it, provides; and he throws this, with careless opulence, into a single aside. Then he returns to the upbuilding of *his* Shylock.

Note the next turn the scene takes. From the snuffling depreciation of his present store, for his own wonted fawning on these Christian clients, Shylock unexpectedly rises to the dignities of

> When Jacob grazed his uncle Laban's sheep . . .

And with this the larger issue opens out between Gentile and Jew, united and divided by the scripture they revere, and held from their business by this tale from it—of flocks and herds and the ancient East. Here is another Shylock; and Antonio may well stare, and answer back with some respect—though he recovers contempt for the alien creature quickly enough. But with what added force the accusation comes:

> Signior Antonio, many a time and oft
> In the Rialto you have rated me. . . .
> You called me misbeliever, cut-throat dog,
> And spit upon my Jewish gaberdine. . . .

The two Venetians see the Ghetto denizen again, and only hear the bondman's whine. But to us there is now all Jewry couched and threatening there, an ageless force behind it. They may make light of the money bond, but we shall not.

Shakespeare keeps character within the bounds of story with great tact; but such a character as this that has surged in his imagination asks more than such a story to feed on. Hence, partly at least, the new theme of Jessica and her flight, which will give Shylock another and more instant grudge to satisfy. It is developed with strict economy. Twenty-one lines are allowed to Jessica and Launcelot, another twenty or so to her lover and their plans; then, in a scene not sixty long, Shylock and his household are enshrined. As an example of dramatic thrift alone this is worth remark. The parting with Launcelot: he has a niggard liking for the fellow, is even hurt a little by his leaving, touched in pride, too, and shows it childishly.

> Thou shalt not gormandize
> As thou hast done with me. . . .

But he can at least pretend that he parts with him willingly and makes some profit by it. The parting with Jessica, which we of the audience know to be a parting indeed; that constant calling her by name, which tells us of the lonely man! He has looked to her for everything, has tasked her hard, no doubt; he is her jailer, yet he trusts her, and loves her in his extortionate way. Uneasy stranger that he is within these Venetian gates; the puritan, who, in a wastrel world, will abide by law and prophets! So full a picture of the man does the short scene give that it seems hardly possible we see no more of him than this between the making of the bond and the climacteric outbreak of passion upon Jessica's loss and the news of Antonio's ruin.[12]

References to him abound; Shylock can never be long out of our minds. But how deliberate is the thrift of opportunity we may judge by our being shown the first effect of the loss on him only through the ever-useful eyes of Salarino and Solanio. This is politic, however, from other points of view. Look where the scene in question falls, between Morocco's choice of his casket and Aragon's. Here or hereabouts some such scene must come, for the progress of the Antonio and Shylock story cannot be neglected. But conceive the effect of such a tragic outcry as Shylock's own,

> So strange, outrageous, and so variable...

—of such strong dramatic meat sandwiched between pleasant conventional rhetoric. How much of the credibility of the casket story would survive the association, with how much patience should we return to it? But Salarino and Solanio tone down tragedy to a good piece of gossip, as it becomes young men of the world to do. We avoid an emotional danger zone; and, for the moment at least, that other danger of an inconvenient sympathy with 'the dog Jew'. When Shylock's outbreak of anguish does come, the play is nearer to its climax, Bassanio's choice is about to free Portia's story from its unreality, and his savage certainty of revenge upon Antonio will now depress the sympathetic balance against him.

But, considering the story's bounds, what a full-statured figure we already have! Compare the conventional aside, the statement of the theme, in the earlier scene, the bald

> I hate him for he is a Christian....

with the deluge of molten passion which descends upon the devoted Solanio and Salarino, obliterating their tart humour; compare the theme, that is to say, with its development, mere story with character, and measure in the comparison Shakespeare's growing dramatic power.

In tone and temper and method as well this scene breaks away from all that has gone before. The very start in prose, the brisk

Now, what news on the Rialto?

even, perhaps, Solanio's apology for former

slips of prolixity or crossing the plain highway of talk...

seem to tell us that Shakespeare is now asserting the rights of his own imagination, means, at any rate, to let this chief creature of it, his Shylock, off the leash. And verily he does.

The scene's method repays study. No whirling storm of fury is asked for; this is not the play's crisis, but preparation for it still. Shylock is wrapped in resentful sorrow, telling over his wrong for the thousandth time. Note the repetition of thought and phrase. And how much more sinister this sight of him with the wound festering than if we had seen the blow's instant fall! His mind turns to Antonio, and the thrice told

let him look to his bond.

is a rope of salvation for him; it knots up the speech in a dreadful strength. Then, on a sudden, upon the good young Salarino's reasonable supposition that what a moneylender wants is his money back; who on earth would take flesh instead?—

What's that good for?

—there flashes out the savagery stripped naked of

To bait fish withal: if it will feed nothing else, it will feed my revenge.

Now we have it; and one salutes such purity of hatred. There follows the famous speech—no need to quote it—mounting in passionate logic, from its

He hath disgraced me ... and what's his reason? I am a Jew.

to the height of

> If a Jew wrong a Christian, what is his humility? Revenge. If a Christian wrong a Jew, what should his sufferance be by Christian example? Why, revenge. The villainy you teach me I will execute, and it shall go hard but I will better the instruction.

This is a Shylock born of the old story, but transformed, and here a theme of high tragedy, of the one seemingly never-ending tragedy of the world. It is the theme for a greater play than Shakespeare was yet to write. But if this one cannot be sustained on such a height, he has at least for the moment raised it there.

Solanio and Salarino are quite oblivious to the great moral issue opened out to them; though they depart a little sobered—this Jew seems a dangerous fellow. There follows the remarkable passage with Tubal; of gruesome comedy, the apocalyptic Shylock shrunk already to the man telling his ill-luck against his enemy's, weighing each in scales (love for his daughter, a memory of his dead wife thrown in!) as he is used to weigh the coin which is all these Christians have left him for his pride. It is technically a notable passage, in that it is without conflict or contrast, things generally necessary to dramatic dialogue; but the breaking of a rule will be an improvement, now and then, upon obedience to it. So Shakespeare, for a finish, lowers the scene from its crisis, from that confronting of Christian and Jew, of hate with hate, to this raucous assonance of these two of a kind and mind, standing cheek to cheek in common cause, the excellent Tubal fuelling up revenge.

Such a finish, ousting all nobility, both shows us another facet of Shylock himself (solid figure enough now to be turned any way his maker will) and is, as we saw, a shadow against which the high romance of Bassanio's wooing will in a moment shine the more brightly. Sharp upon the heels of this, he comes again; but once more apocalyptic, law incarnate now.

> SHYLOCK. Gaoler, look to him; tell me not of mercy;
>   This is the fool that lent out money gratis:
>   Gaoler, look to him.
> ANTONIO. Hear me yet, good Shylock.
> SHYLOCK. I'll have my bond; speak not against my bond:
>   I have sworn an oath that I will have my bond.

Verse and its dignity are needed for this scene; and note the recurring knell of the phrases:

> I'll have my bond; I will not hear thee speak:
> I'll have my bond, and therefore speak no more.
> I'll not be made a soft and dull-eyed fool,
> To shake the head, relent, and sigh, and yield
> To Christian intercessors. Follow not;
> I'll have no speaking: I will have my bond.

Here is a Shylock primed for the play's great scene; and Shakespeare's Shylock wrought ready for a catastrophe, which is a deeper one by far than that the story yields. For not in the missing of his vengeance on Antonio will be this Shylock's tragedy, but in the betrayal of the faith on which he builds.

> I've sworn an oath that I will have my bond. . . .

How many times has the synagogue not heard it sworn?

> An oath, an oath. I have an oath in Heaven. . . .

He has made his covenant with an unshakeable God:

> What judgment shall I dread, doing no wrong?

—and he is to find himself betrayed.

It is the apocalyptic Shylock that comes slowly into court, solitary and silent, to face and to outface the Duke and all the moral power of Venice.[13] When he does speak he answers the Duke as an equal, setting a sterner sanction against easy magnanimity—at other people's expense! One could complain that this first appeal for mercy discounts Portia's. To some extent it does; but the more famous speech escapes comparison by coming when the spell of the young doctor is freshly cast on us, and by its finer content and larger scope. Structurally, the Duke's speech is the more important, for it sets the lists, defines the issue and provokes that

> I have possessed your grace of what I purpose;
> And by our holy Sabbath have I sworn
> To have the due and forfeit of my bond. . . .

So confident is he that he is tempted to shift ground a little and let yet another Shylock peep—the least likable of all. He goes on

> You'll ask me, why I rather choose to have
> A weight of carrion flesh, than to receive
> Three thousand ducats: I'll not answer that,
> But say it is my humour. . . .

Legality gives licence to the hard heart. Mark the progression. While the sufferer cried

> The villainy you teach me I will execute, and it shall go hard but I will better the instruction.

with the law on his side it is

> What judgment shall I dread, doing no wrong?

from which he passes, by an easy turn, to the mere moral anarchy of

> The pound of flesh, which I demand of him,
> Is dearly bought; 'tis mine, and I will have it....

and in satanic heroism stands defiant:

> If you deny me, fie upon your law!
> There is no force in the decrees of Venice.
> I stand for judgment. Answer: shall I have it?

There is a dreadful silence. For who, dwelling unquestioningly under covenant of law, shall gainsay him?

It says much for the mental hypnosis which the make-believe of the theatre can induce that this scene of the trial holds us so spellbound. Its poetry adds to the enchantment—let anyone try rewriting it in prose—and the exotic atmosphere helps. But how much more is due to the embroidering of character upon story so richly that the quality of the fabric comes to matter little! Shakespeare, at any rate, has us now upon the elemental heights of drama. He cannot keep us there. Portia must perform her conjuring trick; perhaps this is why he gives Shylock full scope before she arrives. But he brings us down with great skill, manoeuvring character to the needs of the story, and turning story to character's account.

The coming of the young judge's clerk does not impress Shylock. How should it? Little Nerissa! He has won, what doubt of it? He can indulge then—why not?—the lodged hate and loathing he bears Antonio. The Duke is busy with Bellario's letter and the eyes of the court are off him. From avenger he degenerates to butcher. To be caught, lickerish-lipped, by Bassanio; and Gratiano's rough tongue serves him as but another whetstone for savagery! He turns surly at first sight of the wise young judge—what need of such a fine fellow and more fine talk?—and surlier still when it is talk of mercy.

He stands there, he tells them yet again, asking no favours, giving none.

> My deeds upon my head! I crave the law,
> The penalty and forfeit of my bond.

Why does Shakespeare now delay the catastrophe by a hundred lines, and let Portia play cat-and-mouse with her victim? From the story's standpoint, of course, to keep up the excitement a while longer. We guess there is a way out. We wonder what it can be; and yet, with that knife shining, Antonio's doom seems to come nearer and nearer. This is dramatic child's play, and excellent of its sort. But into it much finer stuff is woven. We are to have more than a trick brought off; there must be a better victory; this faith in which Shylock abides must be broken. So first she leads him on. Infatuate, finding her all on his side, he finally and formally refuses the money—walks into the trap. Next she plays upon his fanatical trust in his bond, sets him searching in mean mockery for a charitable comma in it—had one escaped his cold eye—even as the Pharisees searched their code to convict Christ. Fold by fold, the prophetic dignity falls from him. While Antonio takes his selfless farewell of his friend, Shylock must stand clutching his bond and his knife, only contemptible in his triumph. She leads him on to a last slaveringly exultant cry: then the blow falls.

Note that the tables are very precisely turned on him.

> if thou tak'st more,
> Or less, than just a pound, be it so much
> As makes it light or heavy in the substance,
> Or the division of the twentieth part
> Of one poor scruple, nay, if the scale do turn
> But in the estimation of a hair . . .

is exact retaliation for Shylock's insistence upon the letter of his bond. Gratiano is there to mock him with his own words, and to sound, besides, a harsher note of retribution than Portia can; for the pendulum of sympathy now swings back a little—more than a little, we are apt to feel. But the true catastrophe is clear. Shylock stood for law and the letter of the law; and it seemed, in its kind, a noble thing to stand for, ennobling him. It betrays him, and in the man himself there is no virtue left.

> Is *that* the law?

he gasps helplessly. It is his only thought. The pride and power in which legality had wrapped him, by which he had outfaced them all, and held Venice herself to ransom, are gone. He stands stripped, once more the sordid Jew that they may spit upon, greedy for money, and hurriedly keen to profit by his shame.

> I take this offer then; pay the bond thrice,
> And let the Christian go.

Here is Shakespeare's Shylock's fall, and not in the trick the law plays him.

He is given just a chance—would the story let him take it!—to regain tragic dignity. What is passing in his mind that prompts Portia's

> Why doth the Jew pause? Take thy forfeiture.[14]

No, nothing, it would seem, but the thought that he will be well out of the mess with his three thousand ducats safe.

Shakespeare has still to bring his theme full circle. He does it with doubled regard to character and story.

> Why, then the devil give him good of it!
> I'll stay no longer question.

If he were not made to stay, by every canon of theatrical justice Shylock would be let off too lightly; wherefore we find that the law has another hold on him. It is but a logical extending of retribution, which Gratiano is quick to reduce to its brutal absurdity. Here is Shylock with no more right to a cord with which to hang himself than had Antonio to a bandage for his wound. These quibbling ironies are for the layman among the few delights of law. Something of the villainy the Jew taught them the Christians will now execute; and Shylock, as helpless as Antonio was, takes on a victim's dignity in turn. He stays silent while his fate, and the varieties of official and unofficial mercy to be shown him, are canvassed.[15] He is allowed no comment upon his impoverishing for the benefit of 'his son Lorenzo' or upon his forced apostasy. But could eloquence serve better than such a silence?

> PORTIA.  Art thou contented, Jew? What dost thou say?
> SHYLOCK. I am content.

With the three words of submission the swung pendulum of the drama comes to rest. And for the last of him we have only

> I pray you give me leave to go from hence;
> I am not well. Send the deed after me,
> And I will sign it.

Here is the unapproachable Shakespeare. 'I am not well.' It nears banality and achieves perfection in its simplicity. And what a completing of the picture of Shylock! His deep offence has been against human kindness; he had scorned compassion and prayed God himself in aid of his vengeance. So Shakespeare dismisses him upon an all but ridiculous appeal to our pity, such as an ailing child might make that had been naughty; and we should put the naughtiness aside. He passes out silently, leaving the gibing Gratiano the last word, and the play's action sweeps on without pause. There can be no greater error than to gerrymander Shylock a strenuously 'effective exit'—and most Shylocks commit it. From the character's point of view the significant simplicity of that

> I am not well.

is spoiled; and from the point of view of the play the technical skill with which Shakespeare abstracts from his comedy this tragic and dominating figure and avoids anticlimax after is nullified.

## The Return to Comedy

THE tragic interest is posted to oblivion cavalierly indeed. Seven lines suffice, and the Duke's processional departure. The business of the rings is then briskly dispatched, and made the brisker by the businesslike matter of the signing of the deed being tacked to it. Thence to Belmont; and while Lorenzo and Jessica paint its moonlit beauty for us, Balthasar and his clerk have time to change costume and tire their heads again for Portia and Nerissa. They have evidently, as we saw, none too much time; for Launcelot is allowed a last—and an incongruously superfluous—piece of clowning. But the musicians can play ahead for an extra minute or two if hooks and eyes refuse to fasten, and no one will notice the delay. The last stretch of dialogue is lively; a comic quartet coming after the consort of viols, and it asks for a like virtuosity. The play ends, pleasantly and with formality, as a fairy tale should. One may wonder that the last speech is left (against tradition) to Gratiano; but one practical reason is plain. Portia and Bassanio, Antonio, Lorenzo and Jessica must pace off the stage in their stately Venetian way, while Gratiano's harmless ribaldry is tossed to the audience as an epilogue. Then he and Nerissa, now with less dignity than ever to lose, skip quickly after.

## Act-Division and Staging

HOWEVER well the First Folio's five-act rule may fit other plays, and whatever, in Elizabethan stage practice, division into five acts implied, there is ample evidence that *The Merchant of Venice* was meant to be played without an effective break. The scenes, and the padding in them, that give time for Portia and Nerissa to change clothes, are one sign of it. The first of these is padding unalloyed, and very poor padding at that. For the second, Shakespeare finds better and pleasanter excuse; but in part, at least, we owe that charming duet between Lorenzo and Jessica to this practical need.[16]

A case of a sort can be made out for the division in the Folio. Granted five acts, this fourth and fifth are manifest; the beginnings and finishings of the first three make useful milestones in the story, but others every bit as useful could be set up. It is worth noting that this act-division does nothing to elucidate the complex time-scheme of our anxious editors; but the Folio's expert play-divider would be no more bothered by that problem than Shakespeare had been. Nor was he concerned to end his acts memorably; the second leaves Aragon in our minds and the third ends with Jessica and Lorenzo's and the play's worst scene.[17] There might, however, be good enough reason in the Elizabethan theatre for making an act's first scene arresting and for letting its last tail away; for they had, of course, no curtain to lower upon a climax, and after an interval interest would need quick rekindling. No producer today, one hopes, will want to lower a picture-stage curtain at such points. Nor, if he is wise, while his stories are working to their joint crisis will he give us pause to think by what strange leaps in time and space they travel.

But surely there are many signs that—however, for convenience sake, it is to be acted, with or without pause—Shakespeare has conceived and constructed the play indivisibly. There is the alternating between Venice and Belmont, and the spinning-out of the Portia story to fit with the other; neither device gains by or countenances act-division. There is the unhesitating sweep of the action up to the trial-scene, and indeed beyond it. One can parcel it up in various ways—the Folio's and half a dozen others—and on various pleas; but will any one of them make the story clearer; will it not, on the contrary, do something to disclose its confusions? Prose and blank verse, rhymed couplets and a quatrain are used indifferently for tags; so these form no consistent punctuation. There is no scene, not even the trial-scene, that ends with a full close, until the play ends. There is, in fact, no inherent, no dramatic pause in the action at all; nor can any be made which will not be rather hindrance than help to a performance.

Well-paced acting will take the play straight through in the traditional, vague two hours. But if, for the weakness of the flesh, there must be pauses, division into three parts will be a little less awkward than into two. If you do not stop before the trial-scene you cannot, of course, stop at all; the play will be virtually over. You may reasonably pause at the end of the Folio's Act III. This alone, though, will make very unequal division. For an earlier pause, the moment of Bassanio's departure from Venice will serve.[18] This splits the first three acts of the Folio all but exactly in two. Delay the pause another scene and we shall have done with Morocco.

The second part would then begin with the tale of how Shylock took his loss and our first news of Antonio's losses, and would develop this interest till the eve of the trial. Incidentally it would hold all the inordinate time-telescoping; a helpful quickening, this, to its pulse. But these divisions and the choice of them have no other validity than convenience; the play must be thought of as an integral whole.

Needless to say that the confusion of scene-divisions in most modern editions (a very riot of it when Jessica is eloping) is not Shakespeare's; nor is the expert of the Folio responsible, nor even Rowe, who contents himself with marking the moves from Venice to Belmont and back.[19] For a century editors disputed as to when *Venice, a street*, shifted to *A room in Shylock's house*, or to *Another street*, or to *Before Shylock's house*, and chopped up the action and checked its impetus, when one glance at Shakespeare's stage, its doors and balcony and traverses, shows with what swift unity the play and its playing flow on. And whatever picturing of Venice and Belmont a producer may design, this swift-flowing unity he must on no account obstruct. Let that be clear.

But there is little difficulty in the play's production, once its form is recognized, its temper felt, the tune of its verse and the rhythm of its prose rightly caught. The text is very free from errors, there are no puzzles in the actual stagecraft. The music may come from Elizabethan stock, and the costuming is obvious. Nothing is needed but perception and good taste, and from the actors, acting.

## Notes

1  If the effect is one and the same, one might think the question unimportant. But Daniel, making out his three months, is generous of 'intervals', not only between acts, but between

scenes; and even Furness, on his subtler scent, can say, 'One is always conscious that between the acts of a play a certain space of time elapses. To convey this impression is one of the purposes for which a drama is divided into acts.' Therefore an important and a much-disputed question is involved—and begged. And, in practice, the pernicious hanging-up of performances by these pauses is encouraged, to which scenery and its shifting is already a sufficient temptation.

2  See also Preface to *Antony and Cleopatra*.

3  It is, one may say, a commonplace of stagecraft, Elizabethan or other; but none the less worthy for that.

4  And such interest as there is in Aragon's scene is now lessened, perhaps, by our knowledge that Bassanio is on his way; even more, by the talk in the scene before of Antonio's misfortune. But Shakespeare, as his wont is, plucks some little advantage from the poverty of the business by capping Aragon's vapidity with the excitement of the news of Bassanio's arrival.

5  Though there are commentators who maintain that Nerissa—even Portia, perhaps—gives Bassanio the hint to choose lead, or has it sung to him:

> Tell me, where is fancy *bred*,
> In the heart, or in the *head*?
> How begot, how nouri*shed*?

And if he'll only listen carefully he will note that they all rhyme with *lead*.

Shakespeare was surely of a simpler mind than this—his audiences too. And he had some slight sense of the fitness of things. Would he—how *could* he?—wind up this innocent fairy tale with such a slim trick? Besides, how was it to be worked; how is an audience to be let into the secret? Are they likely to tag extra rhymes to the words of a song as they listen to it? Or is Nerissa—not Portia, surely!—at some point to tip Bassanio 'the wink' while he smiles knowingly back to assure her that he has 'cottoned on'? Where, oh, where indeed, are such dramatic fancies bred? Not in any head that will think out the effect of their realization.

6 Little to be found in him, upon analysis, to refute the frigid verdict lately passed upon him by that distinguished and enlightened—but in this instance, surely, most mistakenly whimsical—critic, Sir Arthur Quiller-Couch, of fortune-hunter, hypocrite and worse. Is anything more certain than that Shakespeare did not *mean* to present us with such a hero? If Sir Arthur were producing the play, one pities the actor asked to give effect to his verdict.

7 Possible extra time was needed for the shifting of the caskets and their furniture and the setting of the chairs of state for the Duke and the Magnificoes. But in that case these last must have been very elaborate.

8 For the bearing of this upon the question of act-division, see p. 65.

9 But Rosencrantz and Guildenstern, as Shakespeare wrote them, are not the mere puppets that the usual mangling of the text leaves them.

10 It is worth remarking that the word 'sad', as Shakespeare uses it, may mean rather solemn and serious than definitely miserable.

11 This is one of the ever-recurring small strokes of stagecraft that are hardly appreciable apart from an Elizabethan stage. Shylock and Bassanio are to the front of the platform. Antonio, near the door, is by convention any convenient distance off; by impression, too, with no realistic scenery to destroy the impression. Shylock is left isolated, so isolated that the long aside has all the importance and the force of a soliloquy.

12 And so strange has this seemed to many a producer of the play and actor of Shylock, that we have been given scenes of pantomime in which Shylock comes back from Bassanio's supper to find Jessica flown. The solitary figure with a lantern, the unanswered rapping at the door, has become all but traditional. Irving did it, Coghlan had already done something of the sort, and—I fancy—Booth. An ingenious variation upon a theme by Shakespeare, that yet merely enfeebles the theme. The lengthier elaboration of a Shylock seen distracted at the discovery of his loss is, of course, even more inadmissible, since Shakespeare has deliberately avoided the situation.

13  Upon the modern stage he usually has Tubal for a companion; one has even seen him seconded by a small crowd of sympathetic Jews. How any producer can bring himself so to discount the poignant sight of that drab, heroic figure, lonely amid the magnificence around, passes understanding!

14  See Furness for an elaborate, illuminating and witty comment upon the situation.

15  It is hard to see why Antonio's taking the money to pass on to 'the gentleman that lately stole his daughter' and providing that, for his half-pardon 'he presently become a Christian', should be so reprobated by some critics. If we have less confidence today than had Antonio in the efficacy of baptism, have we none left in the rightfulness of reparation? Not much in its efficacy, perhaps. Antonio, one must insist, does not mean to keep any of the money for himself. One hopes he never lapsed into self-righteousness in recalling this. Nothing is said, however, about the original three thousand ducats!

16  The two scenes are, to a line, of the same length. Add to the one the opening of the trial-scene, and to the other, for safety's sake, twenty bars or so of music, and we have the time allotted for the change of costume.

17  Furness sees dramatic point in the second act ending with Bassanio on the doorstep. I suggest that Nerissa's tag is meant to keep Belmont a little in our minds during the strenuous scene between Shylock and Tubal which follows; but that, if anything, it tells against an act-pause falling here, rather than for it.

18  There is, as we have seen, a possible contracting of the action here that gives a summariness to the last few lines and suggests (to the modern ear, truly) a 'curtain'.

19  Lord Lansdowne's Jew held the stage in Rowe's time; and for this reason, it may just possibly be, he does not trouble to bring the play into closer relation with his own theatre.